Wild Things

Adventures of a Grassroots Environmentalist

Wild Things

Adventures of a Grassroots Environmentalist

Donna Matrazzo

To Eileen,
Enjoy and
preserve our
wild places

Donna Matrazzo

iUniverse, Inc.
New York   Bloomington

Wild Things
Adventures of a Grassroots Environmentalist

Copyright © 2008 by Donna Matrazzo

iUniverse books may be ordered through booksellers or by contacting:

iUniverse
1663 Liberty Drive
Bloomington, IN 47403
www.iuniverse.com
1-800-Authors (1-800-288-4677)

ISBN: 978-0-595-52874-5 (pbk)
ISBN: 978-0-595-62929-9 (ebk)

Printed in the United States of America

Cover photo © Michael Durham

For my mother, Gertrude Puhala Matrazzo,
who showed me strength

It is not enough to describe
the world of nature; the point is
to preserve it. What we need
are heroes and heroines—about a
million of them—willing and able
to fight for the health of the land
and its inhabitants.

Edward Abbey

CONTENTS

Prologue

There were no woods on Wood Street, where I grew up. Nor any birds. Just one block of sooty homes, choked between the railroad tracks and the steel mill. Houses were so close together that if Mom shook the dust mop too far out the hallway window, it was in Mary Mihalko's living room.

From my home now on Sauvie Island, I look out the kitchen window to my own woods, three quarters of an acre. I felt compelled to honor them with a name: Trillium Woods, for the three-petaled wildflowers that bloom by the hundreds each spring. Baking Christmas cookies, I fling open the window to catch the whistling of tundra swans as they fly overhead toward the lake.

Jutting beyond the outskirts of Portland, Oregon, Sauvie is an alluvial isle about the same size and shape as Manhattan. Sparsely-settled farmland graces the southern half. The 12,000 acres of the northern half are protected as a wildlife area by the Oregon Department of Fish and Wildlife. Population count: approximately 445 families and 312 species of wildlife.

I had no idea that when I began to see wild things, really see, that they would take over my life. Not just that I would spend every spare moment hiking, kayaking or bicycling to their wild places. Or knock out my office walls and fill them with windows.

But when the wild things became threatened, I was drawn, or thrust (I'm still not sure which) into the vortex of raging conservation battles. In the challenge of keeping Sauvie Island unchanged, I've changed: I've grown wings of my own.

Over these years I've had the pleasure of getting to know hundreds of grassroots environmentalists. Our story, I realized, is all the same: First comes a deep passion of place. Then the courage to speak up when that place becomes threatened. Then change, and all that change enables.

A friend told me this is a book about empowerment.

I think it's simply about learning how to see.

PART 1
A PASSION OF PLACE

Chapter 1
Four-Mountain Mornings

Out of my driveway I turn northwest, the silhouette of my bicycle pedaling beside me down the narrow country road. To the right, the horizon wears a ruffle of snow-capped Cascade mountains; nearer, along the left, the island and river channel are framed by the velvety folds of the thousand-foot Tualatins. Most mornings I ride the same six miles then back, been doing it for years, every day a different journey. Past migrant workers weeding strawberry fields, past the sign pointing to long-since-gone Fort Williams, past a woman jogging in mango tights, past the cedar barn tipping on its last beams, past plume-bobbing quail scurrying into bushes, past a yellow school bus of surprised faces pressed against dusty windows. I grin and wave.

It's with childlike glee that I allow myself these morning rides, because my childhood was not one of play. For the eldest of four, daughter of a diabetic mother and strict Italian father, Saturdays were not times of leisurely amusement, searching for polliwogs in a pond or admiring the intricate pattern of a butterfly's wings. Instead, they were spent in the gloomy basement with Mom, feeding laundry through the wringer washer, never far from terror that my fingers would be caught and crushed. Our neighborhood had no parks or playgrounds or streams or flowers. I don't recall ever noticing a bird.

Four miles of pedaling pass, then five. Then I hear them. That marvelous joyful trilling, like a class of exuberant French birds learning how to roll their r's. *Rar-r-r-o-o-o. Rar-r-r-o-o-o.* Sandhill cranes, on their spring migration to the Arctic. They're my favorite of all the birds that come to the island, and I squint against the horizon to spot them.

No matter, I know they're there. I pull over to the side and take out my binoculars. Cranes are hard to distinguish in the tall, matted dry grasses, but as they come into view I gasp aloud. In my walks and on my rides around the island, I've seen as many as 55 sandhills at one time. Here, slowly scanning left to right, I count a total of 198.

The sun outlines the long, elegant curve of their backs, these stately silver-grey birds with the brilliant red crown. I watch as some of them walk, necks extended, feet plodding slowly forward like water-filled boots, so unlike their grace in the air. Most of them peck at the earth, digging for earthworms or beetles, tossing dirt aside with their beaks, shoveling holes that nearly bury their heads. When a **V** of Canada geese fly overhead, they look up. Two standing side by side in a seasonal pond preen themselves, fluffing backfeathers with their bills. Four stand at the far end, sentinels, watching.

They're facing northwest, the direction of their summer home in the Arctic, breeding ground for millions of birds. I imagine their flight that brought them to our island today, probably from northern California, following the sparse string of lakes that are all that remain of the disappearing Pacific Flyway.

Three cranes soar in for a landing, their seven-foot wings outstretched. When they near the earth, they pull back, feet out and forward, and gracefully touch down. I watch awhile, but work beckons, so I pedal on. Less than a mile down the road I hear more trilling and see another large flock. This count: 139. I straddle the bicycle, not wanting to stay too long, and catch something out of the corner of my binoculars. Focusing, I realize it's a coyote—the first I've seen on the island—walking around the perimeter of the cranes, staking out a meal.

The earth of Sauvie is nothing like the dirt of Braddock, Pennsylvania. That was mill dust. Grit, really. By this hour on a spring morning, windows opened, I could wipe my palm across the stove and it would be covered with the soot that clung to every surface in town. The mill released clouds that darkened the sky, and Braddock's air would land on me, shiny black particles caught in the soft hairs of my arm, making my skin prickle. "Dirt means work," people would say, as though it were the town's motto. I associated the monstrous blast furnace with death, the early deaths of both my immigrant grandfathers whom I never knew, the horrid leukemias of my uncle and cousin, the man my millworker father saw sliced in half. I always knew I would leave. Where, I had no idea.

As spring edges into summer the landscape is increasingly dotted with seasonal lakes and ponds. Before the first dike was built in the 1920s, the island—bordered on the east by the confluence of the Columbia and Willamette rivers, and on the west by the Multnomah Channel of the Willamette—flooded every year in early summer, and sometimes again later. These lowlands then were wild meadows, full of wapato beds and wildflowers like the lovely, star-shaped violet camas. Native Americans ate the bulbs of both, the women harvesting the wapato with their toes probing down in the mud. Now I watch as these small bodies of water spread across domesticated fields.

Near the end of the road, where pavement turns to dirt, mud nests of cliff swallows encircle the four paned windows of a grey pumphouse. I count 11 nests, and more must be under the cement walkway for I watch scores of the graceful buffy-rumped birds zip in and out from beneath it. Fearlessly they swoop low over me, with their mesmerizing zigzag flight. Zip, to the left. Zip-zip, to the right, mouths gaping, scooping insects, up to 6,000 a day. Rather than flapping their wings up and down, they glide in breaststroke fashion; I think of them as swallowing the air.

Blue skies like this morning's always startle me, because I lived the first decades of my life without ever seeing one. In Braddock the skies were shaded a poisonous brownish stew; snow was never white; nights were without stars. Here the dazzling sapphire of the earth's ceiling still seems to me almost unbelievable, like an amateur painter's improbable view of how beautiful the world could be.

Passing thickets on a dead end road, I stop to marvel at the panorama of the Cascades—the nearly perfect cone of 11,200 foot Mount Hood, next to it Mount Adams, more than a thousand feet higher, and then Mount St. Helens, its snowy crater since the 1980 eruption like a giant's helping of vanilla ice cream with a scoop removed. On such brilliantly clear days Mount Rainier outside Seattle is visible, nearly 200 miles distant. A white-haired woman bicycles past me, wearing a pink sweatshirt decorated with her grandchildren's names. "Beautiful morning, isn't it?" I call out.

"Yep," she smiles in response, "It's a four-mountain morning!"

Foggy days roll in with autumn. Riding along, it's impossible to tell where the pilings enter the water. They seem suspended above the shore's green grass, like O'Keeffe's skulls above the desert. Fog shrouds buildings and drifts off the water. I hear geese overhead, coming closer. Finally two **V**s appear, then vanish in the soft grey air. Sometimes the fog lifts and settles in different places, like an angora blanket moved from bed to bed. Mountains appear and disappear. There is a feeling of romance, of timelessness, traveling over an ocean of clouds. In low fog, trees seem to grow out of the mist.

Bird shows abound; I can't distinguish them except to say they're LBBs—little brown birds. I look up to see a chocolate fireworks of 500 or more birds, flapping their wings in a round shooting cloud. It's over in a few seconds, and they scatter and disappear. Then two groups of about 200 birds each waltz with each other, gracefully swooping and blending, then separating. They land, then all take off again in a repeat performance. In the distance, thousands of birds fly off in perfect unison, swooping together as if to land, then suddenly soaring upward.

Who in Braddock would ever have thought of watching birds, even if there had been any to see? Hiking? Canoeing? Wonderful things a chubby, bespectacled girl could read about in library books were unimaginable in real life, too far beyond the realm of muscled steelworkers, struggling to feed families impoverished from the paycheckless months of union strikes, when even savings bonds from the children's baptisms had to be turned in for cash. As I ventured off on my own—to my family's bewilderment—I sought out people who showed me woods and whitewater, and glimpses of the wild things. More and more fascinated, or merely emerging from a cocoon of experiential deprivation, by small increments over the years I was drawn to wildness, inexorably pulled westward in a search I hardly realized I was making for a place where I might belong.

Through autumn's gentle rains, not unpleasant, I pedaled contentedly in the soft flapping of my bright yellow poncho. Winter rains are different, hard and pelting, driven by fierce headwinds. Tree branches swing wildly, grasses bend sideways from the wind's force. It's hunting season, and men in camouflage clothes pass me in pickups and Broncos. I hear the dull thwap of gunshots, then the sound of air moving in great masses, hundreds of waterfowl lifting off, rising from the wild lands, winging their way toward me.

Along the shore I spot a flash of blue-gray, which I recognize as a belted kingfisher, chattering its rattley *rickety, crick, crick, crick* as it flies down the channel, hunting for small fish.

The belted kingfisher is almost comical-looking with a punk-rock-look double-peaked crest of blue feathers on its large head. From it protrudes a long, dagger-type bill, over a stocky body with short legs and small feet.

Curious, I looked up their story in one of my now-favorite books, Audubon's 1,100-page *Encyclopedia of North American Birds*, and immediately developed a fetish about the kingfisher's feet. A distinguishing feature of kingfishers is syndactylous toes—the outer toes are fused for part of their length to the middle toe. This oddity makes them a relative of some of the world's most charmingly named birds: the Tody family of the Greater Antilles, the Rollers of the East Indies, the Bee-eaters of Africa, the Hoopoe family of Eurasia, and the Motmots of South America.

As winter deepens, temperatures drop, and steel gray ponds speckle the landscape. One morning, 22 degrees, a biting chill snaps at my face and a film of ice crystals covers my gloves. Ice on the road crackles beneath my tires and I pedal carefully, listening as redwing blackbirds whistle their cheery song.

When the daffodils open their blooms, the sandhill cranes return to the same field, the cliff swallows to the same windows of the pumphouse. The sun, the stars, the earth's magnetic field, the smells, the lay of the land instinctively guide them to this place. What, I wonder, is the path of my own flyway? What instinct drew me here? Years ago I stood sobbing on the Mediterranean shore of Santa Eufemia in southern Italy, overwhelmed that my grandmother left the beauty of *le montagne* and *le mare* for the filth and frigid dreariness of Braddock, never once to return. Yet I felt an inkling of understanding, that perhaps somehow I'd inherited an innate desire for water and mountains, for a place with wild things. The first time Mom came to visit Sauvie Island she looked at my life and said, "I don't know how a daughter of mine could have turned out so different. But I can see you belong here."

Chapter 2
The Bald Eagle Watch

At 34 degrees Fahrenheit the February chill feels arctic as we shiver in the parking lot beneath the bridge. Illuminated by the island's only street lamp, Portland Audubon trip leader Mike Houck, his thick black hair unruly at this predawn hour, is already center stage.

"Okay, this bus will leave at 6:30 sharp, so let's start loading up," he intones over the chattering conversations and door slams, heading the bundled crowd toward an off-duty school bus. Forty-two people pile in, toddlers to retirees, dressed unstylishly like me in anything to keep warm: two pair of socks, bunting sweater, hooded rainproof jacket, ear-warmers and two pair of gloves. All except my friend Carolyn Lee. Ever the artist, she's decked out in gold tights, fur-trimmed white boots and a gold-buckled forest green jacket.

At precisely 6:32 the bus drives off. When everyone's settled, Houck balances himself next to the driver and revs his performance into gear. "Okay, how many of you have never seen a bald eagle?" he yells over the rattling motor. Nearly half raise their hands.

My intimacy with the outdoors began with groups like this. At age 22, I'd eked out a journalism degree from Duquesne University through three scholarships, a loan and two jobs, and settled into a city apartment in the Shadyside section of Pittsburgh with my best friend from high school. Downstairs lived a woman who was a member of the

Appalachian Trail Club, and she invited a circle of friends to spend a weekend in a cabin along the trail. It sounded like a party. Instead, I took my first hike, and fell asleep in front of the fireplace.

I hiked all weekend, and felt the kind of fascinating disorientation of a northerner first looking at the southern hemisphere's night sky. There are stars above, but you immediately recognize they're not the ones you've been seeing all your life. I had never walked a distance on anything soft. Hiking down a dip to a stream, I was startled by the drop in temperature, and the way the entire atmosphere seemed to transform. The perfume of a pink flower stopped me in my tracks. Just being in the woods seemed glorious, although I had no idea what anything was called besides Tree, Flower, Rock, Bird.

It's still dark as we unload, snug yet from the bus' warmth, standing in overgrown grass three yards from the road. Houck begins his spiel:

"We started counting eagles ten years ago. Every year they roost in some old growth up there in the Tualatin Mountains…"

"Do you know where they roost?" a hoarse voice queries out of the darkness.

"I've never seen it. I don't even want to know where it is, because I wouldn't want to take the chance of inadvertently giving it away. But consistently—don't ask me why—the bald eagles fly right over this spot. I've seen them late October into mid-April. Seen as many as 40. This year the numbers have been down."

I've been near the eagles' roost in the Tualatin Mountains. Up there, one adult flew so low above me I could hear its wings pumping. Six eagles swooped, creating a wind of their wing power. Following Mike's ethic, I never told anyone. And I never went back.

At first light, Houck points out the eagles' basic flyway.

"There's a sort of butch-haircut-looking stand of trees—see it? To the left of those trees is a knoll. That's where they typically fly over. The last time I was out here there were ten in a group, playing with each other, locking talons."

Houck watches the skies, then suddenly:

"Bald eagle overhead! First one! Okay, that's a young one. Look at the wing, it's not beating rapidly. It's just lumbering overhead. Even though it's high up, you can see it's a really big bird."

"Oop-Oop-Oop-Oop-Oop—there's an adult flying on the left. He's in the blue patch of sky, just below the clouds. Now he's just come over the road cruising left. Oh, now here come two of them playing! Young ones."

"Where?" a woman's voice asks in exasperation.

"Look at the red stand of alder, above the power lines, the tower—see the tower—there are two of them, they're just flying around together, diving. They're just playing. They're getting higher in the air…"

A girl's voice interrupts, "What's this above us?"

"Whoa! An adult, coming high over us, flapping pretty fast. Okay, that's two adults so far. Alr-i-i-ight!"

I cherished those cabin weekends on the Appalachian Trail, and when I was jilted by my first great love, I thought to seek something in nature to fill the emptiness in my life. I found it down the street, in the guise of a youth hostel in Pittsburgh's Squirrel Hill. There was actually no hostel. It was more like a big outdoors club of two rooms, one set up theater-style with creaky folding chairs and another lined with battered canoes and gear. Every Thursday evening some member would present a slide show, and irresistible-sounding day and weekend outings and classes would be announced. Soon I'd blistered my soles with 14-mile hikes. Swamped while whitewater canoeing. Gracelessly fallen hundreds of times learning to telemark ski.

And of course, I needed to be outfitted for these excursions and bought hiking boots, used rental skis, a backpack and wardrobe of heavy wool. To my family, friends and co-workers, this was extraordinarily bizarre behavior. It was as though I'd taken to wearing Halloween costumes to the office. One attractive element was undeniable, though. I'd lost 23 pounds from my five-foot-one-and-a-quarter-inch frame and for the first time in my life could not be described as plump.

And through the people on these adventures I began to learn names: maple tree, mountain laurel, slate, cardinal.

Houck scans the mountains with his binoculars, then stops: "Okay, here comes another one in the middle of the blue patch on the left—it's approaching the road now. That's a young one, no white head. I think that's one of the ones that were playing. Here's one coming right over us. Looks like an adult! Beautiful!"

Carolyn whispers half aloud, "Listen! You can hear him."

The eagle gliding overhead cries out its high-pitched metallic laugh, *kweek-a-kuk-kuk, kac-ka-ka-ka-ka-ka.*

"Mike, why are they flying to Sauvie Island?" a blonde girl asks.

"Eagles are very opportunistic, and in winter on Sauvie there are a lot of dead or dying waterfowl so that becomes their major source of food."

Roger, a man I'd been talking to, calls out, "Here come two overhead on the left."

The blonde girl, whose name is Emily, is ten-and-a-half and jubilant, "I saw his white head! What a perfect view!" Then she notices something else. "What's that?"

Mike spins around. "It's a rough-legged hawk. White head, look for black on the wings. Follow that rough-legged—see where he lands. Maybe we could put a scope on him. We got two more eagles coming over the crewcut spot."

Emily shouts, "Is that the hawk landing in the tree?"

Mike wheels around to check out the tree and confirms, "Emily followed that rough-legged into that tree here. I'm going to put this scope on him." He focuses. "Here's an excellent view of a rough-legged hawk."

After I began to learn the names of things, I realized what I liked best were the stories of things. Sometimes they were stories about the names. It seemed that with any group trip into nature, inevitably talk would turn to wildlife legends, tree mysteries, wildflower love stories and critter dramas great and small. Ever the bookworm and library addict, I bought and borrowed field guides and wildlife books and indulged my curiosity.

So I discovered for myself, for example, that a fox will double back on its own track to outsmart a pursuer. Butterflies can't fly until their wings are warm. Cedar waxwings get drunk on overripe fruit. Pocket gophers have fur-lined pouches on the outside of the face, that they use like shopping bags to carry food back to the burrow. Every now and again on a trip I would surprise myself by saying something that no one else had known.

"Here's the sun!" Carolyn announces as our main hope for warmth slips above Mount Hood, a daybreak extravaganza drawing us from the eagle watch. In the distance, sunglow washes of peach and vermillion streak across the snowy Cascades. Fields in the foreground dotted with cottonwood trees glimmer from dewy green swathes of winter wheat.

Emily is back watching the perched rough-legged and scouts another bird in the tree. Delighted at her new-found spotting skills, she exultantly asks, "What's that bird there at the very top?"

Mike takes a look. "That other bird is a bald eagle. This is a great view. Let's set this other scope lower. We'll make it a short person's scope."

Six-year-old Bobby winks his eye into the scope focused on the eagle. "Cool! Oh, how cool! It looks like the Express Mail box!"

Mike's turned, watching the channel. "Look over here, at these two black birds flying upriver—double-crested cormorants. Look at the light on the young one—the young have a lot of white on the breast…

"Whoa-whoa-whoa-whoa-there's a falcon, an American kestrel, flying over us. It's going to land in this tree. Beautiful! Watch him flick his little tail. I've got him in this spotting scope—he's scratching his little ear!

"What's this? Another kestrel! Another kestrel coming along. Look at its pointed wings. Oh! Oh! What's this? They're mating! There they were! They were mating! Wow! That's pretty groovy!"

The crowd hovers between excitement and disbelief. A woman teases, "We want more proof."

"It *was* pretty quick," Houck admits, then looks back in the scope at the perched falcons. "Look, they're sitting there, contemplating. Well, one has a cigarette. He's preening…"

"Do they stay together?" someone asks.

"Yeah, I think so," Houck answers, then announces for the record, "Two American kestrels were observed mating."

Roger qualifies, "According to Mike Houck."

Sometime past eight the bus appears and now, in daylight, the drive takes on a new timbre. Bags of chocolate chip cookies are passed down the aisle, and we exchange names and snatches of conversation amid Mike's non-stop commentary.

The bus stops near the beginning of Oak Island trail. Half of us are still on the bus and already Houck spots a red-tailed hawk on a utility pole in the distance and has set up both scopes.

"How'd you find that so fast?" Emily asks.

Mike shares his technique: "It's easy. That's where they usually are. I come here often enough and almost always see a hawk there. Another hint is to use your binoculars to scan the treetops first thing when you're bird-watching. You'll often spot hawks and eagles right away."

"What's that sound? Cranes!"

He troops across the turnaround and looks at a hill a few hundred yards away. "Here they are! Sandhill cranes! Let's see—34 of them! Bring those scopes around. A lot of people have trouble telling cranes from herons. They *are* both sort of blue-gray. One distinguishing feature of cranes is their big rump—what did they used to call that in the old days? A bustle. Did everyone get a look?"

I add one of my favorite tidbits about sandhills. "The crane's trilling comes from a windpipe that's as long as five feet, looped like a French horn around its breastbone!"

Mike Houck is Urban Naturalist for the Portland Audubon Society, Director of the Urban Streams Council and number one on my list of local conservation heroes. I've watched him lead groups of mesmerized kids, scopes slung over his athletic, six-foot frame, like some Pied Piper of the city's wilds. He can turn Irish-temper-fierce when fighting against wildlife and habitat destruction, but out in the field his warm blue eyes and bearded smile reflect the generosity with which he shares his wildlife biologist knowledge.

The first I'd seen of him was as a cover guy, when he was featured in the newspaper's glossy Sunday magazine. I found the opportunity to go on one of his nature trips and was amazed that simply standing around watching birds could be so astounding. After that, I tagged along whenever I could.

So I was taken aback one day when he said he had to go out of town, and asked me to replace him leading a Ride on the Wild Side bike ride on the island. "I don't have anything like the depth of knowledge you have," I muttered. "That's a raptor-viewing ride. I can't even tell the difference between a sharp-shinned hawk and a rough-legged hawk."

"Don't worry about it," he said. "Go out and have fun. Share what you know in an entertaining way. And if there's something you don't know, just say so. You'll do it then, I take it? Good."

"Now we're going to hike down a bit through the oaks," Mike directs.

"Why do there seem to be so many different birds along this particular trail?" Marie asks.

"It's the oaks," Mike reasons. "If I had only one tree I could plant for a diversity of wildlife, it would be oaks. You get white-breasted nuthatches, creepers, kinglets…"

He stops, then called "pschee…pschee…pschee…Now listen." A refrain of half a dozen birds responds.

"That's called pishing," he explains. "Pishing throws out sound that attracts a lot of birds like sparrows, towhees, jays. I don't think anyone knows how it works. The birds are hearing a distress call. They come to check out what's distressed—you can get ten, 15 species to come close to you if they're around."

We reach a clearing at the trail's western end, opening onto meadows with Sturgeon Lake beyond. "Okay," Mike chimes in, "Now what bird haven't we seen—what bird would you expect to find right here?" No response, so he furnishes more clues: "Flying low over the ground. White rump."

"Harrier hawk," I guess.

"Right!" Mike confirms. "I don't believe this—look—there's one right now. See how he's harrying his prey?"

"What do you mean, 'harrying'?" Laura asks. "Pishing him off?"

Back in the bus headed to the parking lot, a toddler sleeps, wrapped in a blanket. Bobby's eyes are closed, head slumped on his dad's shoulder. Emily darts her binoculars from tree to passing tree.

"I'd say we had a great day!" Mike encapsulates. "Twenty-one eagles sighted. Sandhill cranes, rough-legged hawks, red-tailed hawks, northern harriers, dozens of songbirds, and let's not forget mating American kestrels.

"But I'm really disappointed in your group. You didn't ask the one question everyone asks: Why'd we have to come out at 6:30 in the morning? Why couldn't we wait until dusk, and watch them fly back to the mountains?"

"Good question," Carolyn agrees, munching on the last of the cookies. "I'm really not a morning person. Why *did* we come out at 6:30?"

Mike's quick with the response. "I think the answer is: they fly out from one spot. But they'd fly back from locations all over the island. It would be problematic, I think, to try and see them at any other time. I've never come out at dusk, to be honest. But if you do, let me know what you see."

Chapter 3
Not Lost but Not Found

Nissa, our springer spaniel, maneuvers into a space among the paddling gear in the back of our Subaru wagon. My husband Bob Stephens and I, sea kayaks loaded, follow the big-wheeled pickup of our friend Howard Blumenthal halfway around the island, down the right fork of the dirt road to our regular put-in at Oak Island.

Winter rains have made the water high, and we're surprised at the day's strong winds that whip its surface into breaking waves. We decide to cut directly across the lake, which forces us to paddle parallel to the breakers, making our long, narrow boats easier to swamp. I'm especially nervous, since this is the first outing in my new Arluk IV sea kayak. Our old two-person boat was wide and beamy. The Arluk has an unfamiliar feel and seems tippy. As we cut across the watery expanse, each approaching wave jolts me back and forth with its passing.

My nervousness is compounded when I realize that with Nissa riding in the back hatch, it's not sealed and I hadn't thought about rear flotation. If I did keel over, my new boat would sink to the bottom of the lake.

Bob grew up in northern Idaho, but has lived mostly in Portland since his teens. Eleven years ago we met at a video conference in Texas. I was a scriptwriter for a scientific company, and he a video producer for a truck manufacturing firm. One afternoon he was in the audience of a workshop where I gave examples of using creativity to imaginatively treat topics like inductively-coupled argon plasma spectroscopy. That evening headed to a barbecue dinner, we reached the hotel elevator at the same time, recognized each other, started talking, and didn't stop the rest of the conference. Tall, bearded, blue-eyed and handsome, an outdoorsman in a business suit, he was unlike any guy I'd ever met in Pittsburgh.

He invited me to Portland for a visit, and took me to the great gorge of the Columbia River, canoeing on a remote mountain lake, and on drives through the city hills where forests opened to reveal expansive vistas of the Cascades, still snow-covered in mid-summer. I wanted a life with both the man and the place.

As we round the bend at Coon Point into a hidden inlet, I'm stirred with anticipation, not just for the sheltered waters and break from the wind. This is the time of year for bird spectacles, if the day is lucky. I've counted as many as 5,000 birds on Sturgeon Lake in a morning. Hanging in the air, blending with the drips of the paddle, has been a low amorphous murmur, punctuated by the circus-clown *QUACK Quack quack quack* of female mallards. The indistinct sound speaks of nature and I've heard it before, never quite the same, and though it might be the wind through the trees, or the water roiling back upon itself, I suspect it is the chattering conversations of great flocks of waterfowl.

We enter the inlet slowly without paddling, the force from our previous strokes waning into a slow glide. I set my paddle down across the boat's coaming, pull out my binoculars and take a look. To the left I count about a thousand snow geese, magnificent white birds with black-tipped wings, in two large separate flocks so thick that the water appears striped with white.

Mallards, about 400 of them, are dabbling just ahead. Almost intermingled are nearly 800 Canada geese. And strung out before us with their long distinctive pointed tails float more than 700 pintails.

Near the headwaters of the Gilbert River we stop for lunch at Howard's favorite spot, a place with tree trunks felled all around. Their stumps are sculpted with a finely honed design, thousands of perfect chisel marks each the size of a beaver's tooth.

Howard's a construction worker, slim and bearded, with powerful arms from his combined nail-pounding and paddling. For 15 years he's been exploring the island's waters and knows every hole, wash and slough. As a trip leader for our local kayak club, he's become so familiar with people and their boats that once, on a weekend trip, he recognized who was driving into camp at night by their headlights' reflection on the boat bottom.

Today Howard shows us a back route with calm waters through sloughs and marshes. Coming to the end of a man-made channel, he directs us to a spot straight ahead and says to paddle to that point, then turn left onto the main body of the lake. He and Bob gunkhole along the channel's edges while I surge ahead.

After paddling for 20 minutes without reaching the point, I realize I don't see any point anymore. The place I'm heading toward looks just like another bend in the continuous meandering shoreline and I can't distinguish where I'm supposed to be headed. Looking back, I see Bob far behind me and can't spot Howard at all.

Ahead of me there's a boy playing in a kayak next to shore in front of a gravel boat ramp. Cars are parked close together, but I don't see ours. This can't be our put-in; I haven't yet come to the big open area of the lake.

Now Bob's not behind me anymore. It's late, past four, and it will start to get dark in an hour. I have no idea where I am. Had I been going the wrong way all along? Did Bob eventually realize it and turn around? But why didn't he call to me, or blow his whistle?

This route has a strong tailwind, so I know I've gone a hefty distance and there's no question of turning back now. I also understand the immensity of the lake and realize I could be anywhere. I scan the tree-lined shore for some hint, some building, something familiar, but there's nothing.

I paddle on, knowing that eventually I'll reach a recognizable put-in. Now it's 4:30. What's that gate ahead?

The landfall has a familiar look about it. When I get out of the boat and walk up on the dike I realize I'm at the Narrows, a portage into Steelman Lake, our favorite put-in. Nissa leaps out and I drag the boat up over the dike and into the narrow section leading to Sturgeon's West Arm, then farther west in to Steelman. I've been here many times, although never alone, but I'm certain I can find my way home from here and that Bob and Howard will be waiting for me when I finally reach Steelman's put-in.

My confidence wanes as I paddle out of the Narrows into what should be the West Arm, where there should be a stand of snags, almost like pilings. There's nothing, and I wonder whether the high water has submerged the stumps, because the place feels right. I keep paddling, hunting for the fence in the water and the small island that should be there. I spot them both. This is it!

Nissa and I jump out of the kayak onto shore and half-run uphill to the road. No one's there for me. It's 5 o'clock and will soon be dark.

Inside a parked car, a man wearing a top hat sits with a rotund woman and a small yelping dog. Why is no one here to meet me? Where are they? They should have been back hours ago. They saw me paddling on ahead; there aren't that many places I could have gone. Howard knows these waters so well.

I'm more than six miles from home, with a 55-pound loaded kayak, down a dead end road where now I recall that a woman was killed. It's 5:10.

It begins to rain. The dog and the man in the top hat get out of the car. He has a whip, which he thwacks against the ground, over and over, while the dog yelps nearby. The woman slides out; she's almost as round as she is tall, wearing a long slick black cape. Occasional cars and pickups loaded with gun racks pass by, occupied all by men; a few of them slow down to look. The sun has set and it's getting dark.

Enough, I think. This caped and top-hatted couple may seem bizarre, but they're driving a Volkswagen Rabbit, there's only one road out of here, and how can they steal my new kayak? I memorize the license number while I pull the Arluk behind a fence overgrown with grasses, and stash the paddle and life jacket in the front hatch. Everything else I stuff into the little gym bag I'll carry on my shoulder.

Rain falls steadily as Nissa and I leave the gear and begin walking down the road. With each passing vehicle comes promise and dread. It could be Howard or Bob, or it could be someone who might force me into a car.

I'm wearing good rain gear, but my feet hurt in the rubber boots. They have no cushions on the sole, and I try not to think about the blisters forming, or the rain, or how tired I am, or the nagging ache of where everyone else might be. I imagine I'm walking quickly, but in 45 minutes I come to the county line and know there are still five miles to go.

After an hour and a half, despite it all, I begin to enjoy the walk. It's a warm evening, with springtime smells of the earth, frogs croaking heartily and hordes of geese squawking as they lift off. I'm thankful for Nissa and her companionship.

The cars are less frequent; I watch each one. A pickup approaches with a kayak on the roof—it's Howard! I yell and wave as he continues down the road, then backs up and stops. We help Nissa climb into the rear and I stumble wearily into the front seat. He drives down to Steelman. The lakeshore is empty, the kayak's there, untouched, and I help load it onto the roof rack.

As we drive back to Oak Island, Howard fills me in. Bob's still at the Oak Island put-in. It seems I had it all right and all wrong. I was going the right way, but paddled beyond the put-in. That was where the boy had been kayaking. Bob didn't call to me because he thought perhaps I wanted to paddle more. When he and Howard realized I'd missed the spot, I was too far ahead for them to yell or catch up.

Bob watched me through the binoculars, saw me drag the kayak over the dike into the Narrows, and figured with the wind behind me I'd be headed to the familiar spot at Steelman.

It's nearly 8 o'clock when Howard and I arrive at Oak Island. Bob sits waiting in the car, its headlights directed out on the lake in case I had turned around and paddled back— spotlights to guide me home.

Chapter 4
Jewels of the Flyway

Bob and I lived in a small 1920s bungalow in the Laurelhurst section of Portland, on a street canopied with maples. From there we hiked, bicycled and kayaked our way around the region, but the place we were most drawn to was Sauvie Island. After one paddling trip we stopped at a garage sale. The house was on the market and we were both struck with the notion of how wonderful it would be to live on the island.

We spoke of it on and off for a few years, then one July Sunday in 1988 three For Sale signs spurred us to action. Tuesday evening a real estate agent showed us the two houses we could afford. There was a shabby one on three acres, and a remodeled cedar-sided ranch on an acre and a half of land, half of it lush woods, across the road from a mile-long forest surrounding a lake. In less time than it takes me to decide on a new dress, I knew this was it. At eight the next morning we phoned with an offer.

From out of somewhere an idea had taken hold of me during the night, when I couldn't sleep for imagining myself in the place. So our offer included a contingency that the sellers, who had remodeled the 40-year-old house, would knock out the two walls that faced the woods in the room that would be my office. We replaced them with windows to wildlife.

That autumn, we set about creating an official National Wildlife

Federation backyard wildlife habitat—our very own stop on the west's major migratory bird route, the Pacific Flyway. Bird feeders, bird baths and birdhouses set the stage for an ever-changing performance of more than three dozen species, including red-breasted nuthatches, pileated woodpeckers, pine siskens, Stellar's jays, evening grosbeaks, western tanagers, even an egret.

Now binoculars hang in every room, a spotting scope on a tripod stands ready next to the refrigerator. Meals, discussions, garden projects are all punctuated with gasps at the goings-on outdoors. The air sings in layers of songs, and a daily drama unfolds of wild lives and loves, flights, dances, births and deaths.

Take, just for example, the jewels of the flyway, the hummingbirds.

As they whizzzz! flash! zip! outside my office window, I'm convinced that hummers were the models for those '50s sci-fi flicks of aliens and their space ships. The motions, I observe, are perfectly mimicked: A shape rising into the scene from below a window ledge. Hovering, watching. Another suddenly appears. They chatter that high-pitched alien jabber. Then— zip!—they're gone—disappeared into the airspace of the universe.

It's Sunday afternoon and Howard, Bob and I, and our 7-year-old goddaughter Malina McKenzie, are eating lunch in the kitchen, watching hummingbirds vie for positions at the window feeder.

"I've heard," I mention off-handedly, "that if you hold red bee balm flowers in front of your face and stand perfectly still, hummingbirds will fly right up to you."

"Oh yeah?" Howard laughs, in a few seconds adding, "Let me try something." He trounces outside in his heavy boots, startling the hummers as he takes the feeder from its hook and holds it motionless. In a few minutes four of the whirlybirds return, darting around him, one landing near his nose.

"I want to try!" Malina erupts with excitement. Three hummingbirds buzz over almost immediately. Malina stands there, with unchildlike patience, until her arms tire. Back inside she whispers, "I could feel the wind from their wings."

Mid-January I begin to envision phantom hummers, so anxious am I for their return, although it will certainly be another month, most likely two. I was 35 when I saw my first hummingbird, twittering from one ruby hibiscus to another beneath the balcony where I sat reading at dawn in Cozumel, Mexico.

Those hummers flitting in Mexico's winter sun are the same birds who come to feed at our northwest gardens from March through August. I fly, white-knuckled, in a 50-ton silver tube a mile above the earth while that one-tenth of an ounce of sapphire feathers and bone transports its four-inch body over a similar distance.

Hummingbirds return faithfully to the same place each year. I didn't know that on March 26th, my second spring on Sauvie. I stood talking on the phone near my desk, marveling at flocks of redwing blackbirds and evening grosbeaks. Suddenly a glimmer caught my eye, and I noticed a hummingbird, hovering anxiously at the exact spot, now empty, where I'd had a feeder the previous summer. This bird had flown, perhaps, from its winter home in southern Mexico, over the turquoise Bay of Campeche, over the ancient ruins of Teotihuacan, past palm trees of San Diego county, above the Mohave Desert (possibly the very day that desert wildflowers burst into bloom) beyond the Sierra Madres, up the San Juaquin Valley, around Mount Shasta, over the Siskiyou Mountains and through the Willamette Valley to precisely the middle of my side office window. I excused myself from the phone call: "I have to go outside and feed a guest."

The following spring I was ready, so I thought. Sunday, March 10th, two weeks earlier than the previous year, I took all six feeders from the back cupboard of the pantry and filled them, carefully measuring the four-to-one nectar of water and sugar. I suspected I was again late, as first thing Monday a rufous hummer came flitting by the window.

The Multnomah County Library allows a card-holder to check out 150 books at a time. One spring I borrow a stack of hummingbird books, the reader's version of a wildlife film festival.

Amongst those pages of lore, I learn that maybe sci-fi filmmakers didn't pattern their work after hummers, but inventor Igor Sikorsky did. The rotors of his helicopter are based on the hummingbird's singular avian ability to hover and fly backwards. Hopi Indians danced in Rain Bird costumes to celebrate the tiny bird's return as flowers bloomed with the first desert rains. Hummingbirds were honored as the souls of long-dead ancestors by the Chayma tribe of Trinidad. In 1519 Raphael painted hummingbirds on the Vatican loggia. Anne de Belle Massena, the 19th century French duchess for whom Anna's hummingbird is named, kept a magnificent collection of hummingbird skins displayed in her palace.

I come to appreciate that we're fortunate to see hummingbirds at all. North and South America are the only places on earth where wild hummingbirds fly free. When Europeans first came to the Americas, they were so captivated by the tiny marvels that they collected their skins by the tens of thousands to adorn hats and dresses. No one will ever know how many species may have been obliterated. Of the remaining 300 or so, about 20 reach the United States, and four—black-chinned, Anna's, calliope and rufous—migrate to the northwest.

Bob and I sit side by side behind the kitchen table, like tourists at a sidewalk cafe, and watch the hummingbird show. Rascal Rufous is the star this evening. From his perch on a middling branch of the hemlock tree, he guards all twelve holes of the kitchen-window feeders. Any time another hummer flies near, zip! he charges to attack it mid-flight, then zip! dashes back to the same spot on his branch. Again. Again. With great amusement, we focus our binoculars to track his maneuvers and count more than 20 times the rufous has chased off an intruder. Every third or fourth assault he pauses to feed himself, a kingly guzzling, monitoring the skies with each sip. As dusk falls, he disappears into the woods.

It's serious work, I've found, this hummingbird feeding. The whirring bird's metabolism and circulatory system are voracious. The heart rate of a blue-throated hummingbird in flight is 1,200 beats per minute. There's no time to rest. Continually hungry, a hummer will daily consume as much as 70 percent of its body weight. For a human my size, than would mean 85 pounds of food per day.

By April, when our backyard's full entourage of hummers has arrived, my office windows host a non-stop feeding frenzy. Because each bird's gorget, or throat pattern, is different, I once tried to track them. I numbered each one, drew its pattern and gave it a description: #1. Stripes on neck, stripe and feather aberrations on chest. #2. Dark pattern on neck with more dark spots on right side. #23. Only one leg. Number three had a gorgeous orange gorget, but was out-glittered by #11, whom I nicknamed The Flasher. His shimmering orange-red gorget blazed from chin to chest. No wonder females are attracted.

It is my observation, although I've not seen it verified in field guides, that female hummingbirds feed in a manner different from males. While jabbering males attack each other with ferocity, stabbing with their long sword-like beaks until the other birds are chased away, females seem to graciously joust for position, politely moving in and out of the feeding spaces. By my count, with four pages of notes, the 26 birds fed a total of 73 times in my one hour of tracking. When undisturbed, a hummingbird might drink as many as 48 sips at a time; when attacked, one or two had to suffice.

I am mesmerized. On the perching feeders, the hummer's unimaginably tiny feet grasp the small rung; sometimes its body trembles with each sip. When the hummingbird is finished and lifts its head, nectar glistens at the tip of its beak. On the clear plastic feeders there is no perch, and the birds must continue to hover while they eat, offering a front-row view of their remarkable muscular wings, structured almost like a hand, sweeping fluidly in a figure-eight. When the nectar is low, the hummer's long, slender tongue reaches down to the last drops. Hummers fly from trees to feeder as we eat outdoors, buzzing fearlessly around us, whirring like miniature dentist drills through the air.

What a difference, I stop and think, from my only recollection of birds from my youth in Braddock. When I was ten, I was one of the Saint Michael's Grade School students selected by Sister Philippa to be part of a contest at Pittsburgh's Carnegie Museum of Natural History. Saturdays I would take the streetcar for an hour into town, checklist in hand of the multitude of birds and animals I was to learn to recognize. I remember standing at the glass displays of stuffed birds, futilely trying to distinguish one from the other, attempting desperately to arouse some interest on my part in these dull lifeless objects. Although it broke my heart to let down our school, I realized it was impossible for me and I quit. Sometimes now I wonder if any of those stuffed birds were hummers.

When the nights turn frigid, hummingbirds go into a torpor, a state of mini-hibernation. They dramatically lower respiration, heartbeat, body temperature and oxygen consumption to reduce the need for food and warmth.

Biologists consider hummers tropical birds who come north for a certain part of the year. But those who judge life by home and hearth might say they live here, where they mate and nest. Lacking a magnificent song, the male courts the female with acrobatics. Now that I know what to listen and look for, when I'm outdoors in spring I'll recognize small particular notes of chatter that precede the male's mating aerial dance of swoops, darts and rapid deep dives. His tiny body is precisely angled to reflect the sun.

Male hummingbirds are labeled "promiscuous" in the birding world. After mating once, a male will head off to find another female, and another, as many as possible during the mating season. The female is left alone to build the nest, bear chicks and rear the brood.

A hummingbird nest is a mastery of camouflage. Although there must be many in our woods, I've only seen one in all these years, and that was by accident. Helping me clear a trail that first autumn, a friend's daughter spotted a nest on branch I'd cut. The female spends five days creating a well-disguised two-inch home for her young. First she'll find a hidden spot, perhaps under a leaf or in the crotch of a branch. She'll gather spider webs, plant down and moss, weave them into a cup shape, then mask the concoction with a cover of lichens or bark. The two eggs she'll lay are the smallest eggs in the world, but quite immense for her; she is only eight times the weight of each. The two eggs are laid in intervals of a few days, then, depending on the species, she incubates them for 11 to 17 days. The newborns are miniscule, without feathers. In half a week they open their eyes; in a week, their feathers are well-sprouted. She feeds regurgitated nectar and insects, some stolen from spiders' webs, into their craws. In three weeks, the young are full-feathered beauties, ready to fly on their own.

Chee…Chee…Chee…Chee…

Hearing the sound, I press my forehead against the kitchen window and spot the fledgling hummingbird at the side of the deck, crying out, its beak opening wide with each effort. Two adults probe at the feeder, ignoring it. I recall that a few years ago a fledgling hummer, crying in the middle of our yard, had allowed me to lift it and move it to safety. So I go outside, intending to cradle this hungry baby bird in my hands and gently set it on the feeder. As I approach, it flies there on its own; I come inside to watch.

The young bird fluffs out, transforming layers of feathers into air pockets that hold in warmth. Although it's mid-May there's a chill to the air. The fledgling's feathers are soft and new-looking, with white underparts. Its eyes are black, with dark feathers beneath its chin. Rocking precariously on the feeder's perch, off-balance, it cries at the adults feeding, beak open, desperately trying to get their attention. They ignore it. The fledgling obviously doesn't have a clue about drinking from this plastic and glass contraption. It's sitting *between* two of the plastic flowers that encircle the feeding holes.

Adults come and leave around the fledgling, but none moves to help. The young bird watches, then tries to imitate them, poking its beak hard into the red plastic, again and again. Finally it moves over and pecks inside a flower, finds the hole and begins drinking the sweet nectar. I can almost feel its delight at the discovery. The fledgling submerges its beak deep into the flower and sucks hard, guzzling, its body quivering. It sucks and sucks and sucks. An adult lands, and even though other feeding spots are empty, it stabs the fledgling on top of the head; the young one doesn't take notice.

By late afternoon when Bob gets home from work, the fledge has been sated more than once, and we watch it become a more skillful acrobat as it veers back and forth between the deck, feeder and apple tree. One time it gets confused and flies headlong into the red ribbon from last year's Christmas wreath. The following day is Saturday; we indulge ourselves with hours of watching its quenchless feeding. In the week following, it plumps out, not fluffed from the feathers, but rotund from overeating. In another week, we cannot see it. Whether it has become a proper weight and we don't recognize it, or whether it's gone, we'll never know.

Soon the flowers are in full bloom. Hummingbirds prefer them to the feeders, and drink nectar from the impatiens outside the dining room door. The blue delphiniums and red nasturtiums in the vegetable garden. Bee balm. Foxgloves. Fuchsias. Geraniums. Lilies. Nicotinias. Petunias. There is a view of flowers, and hummingbirds, from every window.

Long before the last blooms fade, the hummingbirds take their leave, almost imperceptibly, until by August's end, they've all gone. Time to give the feeders a final cleaning, and tuck them far back on the pantry shelf for six months, when once again the fresh sweetness of spring washes through the air.

We're talking hummingbirds, my friend Marcia Hoyt and I, as we hike along the trail at Virginia Lakes, the state park across the road. I tell of a naturalist who said that when her hummingbird feeders run dry, the birds come and peck at her window.

Marcia says, "I have an even better one. There's a house about three doors up from mine. One year it was warm and the hummingbirds came back early. Then suddenly there was a cold snap. The woman who owns the house saw three hummingbirds shivering outside her kitchen window. She opened it and the birds flew in. They stayed there, flying around her kitchen for a week, until the weather changed. Isn't that marvelous? I tried for years to buy that house."

Chapter 5
Unto Dust

I lace up my mud boots, lock the front door and stuff my greying curls inside a soft angora hat. Death walks with me today. Crossing the road, I pass neighboring houses and turn into the woods of Virginia Lakes. I've just returned from my father's funeral. Through the ordeal, 2,500 miles away, I longed for these woods, for the solace and soul and clear-headedness they bring to me.

Friday two weeks ago, October, 1990, Dad collapsed from a massive heart attack and I flew home to Braddock, knowing that with him still in a coma after 24 hours, the prognosis was not good. Mary Jane, my younger sister, picked me up at the airport; it was nearly midnight.

"Do you want to go to the ICU and see him? They'll let us in."

No! I ached inside.

"Yes," I answered, trying to numb my dread.

No matter how I'd prepared myself, how I'd braced myself, I saw an unfamiliar old man, hair nearly white, a corpse with air blasted seven rushes a second into an inanimate body, his swollen face smeared across the pillow, tube-bruised lips connected to a machine flashing uncaring numbers that spoke of all that was left of his life.

I kissed him and held his hand, half cold, and said I was there, and that I loved him. Mary Jane left the room. His eyes slowly opened, covered with a milky film, rolled back into his head. Mary Jane had said this might happen and it was only an involuntary reflex, but I wanted to believe, did believe, that something deep inside had heard me, and he knew I had come for him.

What do you say to your father in a coma? I babbled on about Bob and our new puppy we named Jibo and news of Oregon friends he'd met, interspersed with declarations of love and wishes that he felt comfortable.

"I'm ready to go," I eventually called to Mary Jane, and Dad looked up again. That was the last time I saw his eyes open.

The scene is vivid in my mind as I walk into the thick part of the woods, a carpet of browning leaves crinkling beneath my shuffle. Lichens hang from the bare winter branches of a massive old cottonwood, its corrugated grey-brown trunk brilliant with bright green moss. Untypical for Oregon's soggy Novembers, the sky is a clear azure today, crows cawing incessantly overhead. Sunlight streams in ribbons across huge fallen logs. They're called nurse logs, and from their death other life springs—new trees take root, ferns and mushrooms burst forth, animals find sanctuary in their eroding cavities.

Mom and my two brothers arrived and the five of us sat down with the doctor. He estimated that Dad had been without oxygen to the brain for 12 to 16 minutes; four to six minutes usually leaves a person brain-dead. By Sunday, he'd been in a coma 48 hours. The lack of signs of improvement was not encouraging. An EEG, or brain scan, would be ready the next day.

It became a world of disbelief, that Dad wouldn't ever come home again. We sobbed alternately in explosive bursts. Mary Jane looked for Dad's car keys in the dining room credenza and found a Christmas card Dad had already bought, "To My Wife."

I take the side path to a footbridge overlooking the marsh. Virginia Lakes are seasonal, gone in summer, spilling across the meadows with winter and spring rains. A small portion is flooded and I scan it with my binoculars, delighted to see eight mergansers and a flock of 29 widgeon. I watch in stillness as they dive for food, their white rumps glinting in the winter sun. Off in the distance, a great blue heron stands patiently, then takes off with a loud sqwark. The heron's species is nearly 60 million years old and its distinctly pterodactyl shape evokes a timelessness in the skies and mountains beyond.

The EEG results were in: Dad's brain activity was very minimal and a second test would be performed in two days. If it showed he was totally brain-dead, the respirator would be turned off. If not, Pennsylvania law allows "terminal weaning," a continual lowering of the respirator's rate until nature takes over. The doctors and our family agreed we would consent to that. It was November 4th, Mom's birthday, and we hoped Dad would pull through at least another day.

I sit for awhile at the top of the footbridge, the sun warm against my back. Two Canada geese honk noisily overhead. Blackberries form a hedgerow around the marsh; in August we hike with baskets and turn the juicy berries into fresh cobblers topped with whipped cream. Getting up to leave, I hear tundra swans and search the sky as I spot their elegant, graceful flight.

The second EEG showed extremely miniscule brain activity. When the neurologist examined Dad, one pupil responded slightly to light. That was it. And so the respirator was turned down, from seven breaths per minute to four. No change. But at some point, in five minutes, or five days, there would be. I rubbed Dad's arm. He was breathing, his flesh was warm. His mind was gone. But how easy, how selfish, it would be, to keep the respirator going. To keep him breathing, keep him warm. To keep him there for me to hold.

The family priest had assured Mom that in the eyes of the Catholic Church, Dad had died with the heart attack. The respirator was artificial life. When the priest left, Mom asked "Where is Dad's soul?" to no one in particular. "I think he's in Limbo," I said, referring to the place that's neither heaven nor hell, where Catholics believe the souls of unbaptized children remain for all eternity. "His body has to die for his spirit to rest in peace."

I stared out the window, more conscious than ever that Braddock is devoid of the woods and wildlife that I'd come to love and live around since I moved away. Taking Dad off the respirator, letting the life seep from him, seemed to me not a decision to be made in a high-gloss-linoleum hospital room, but in the fresh air under a cathedral canopy of trees. I squinted at a bird sitting on a roof. It was probably a pigeon, but I imagined it a red-tailed hawk, and that I was thinking things through back in the raw spiritual wildness of the Northwest woods.

While the respirator gave Dad two breaths a minute, he surprised everyone by taking enough small breaths on his own to keep his heart beating strong.

Suddenly Dad began to gasp, deep gasps that caused his heartbeat to escalate from 62 to 108, the EKG line a wild jagged pattern dancing across the screen. We watched in horror as he seemed to be suffocating himself, taking deep powerful gasps, sometimes with such force to lift his head clear off the pillow. His cheeks and forehead were flushed and taut from the effort.

This is it, we thought, and crowded around him, rubbing his hands.
"You can go, Dad."
"It's okay."
"Grandma's waiting for you."
"We love you."
"It's okay to go, Dad."
But Dad, the steelworker and one-time boxer, had strength enough to continue on. Eventually the machine was turned off as had been agreed, although Dad kept gasping for breath. One by one we quieted, and just held him, telling ourselves he didn't feel anything. I silently wished to go back to the slow, gentle respirator, and tried to find peace in my heart to match the rational thoughts of our decision.

After a while the mucous built up in his lungs and gave him a gurgling rasp with each breath. "Baba called that a death rattle," Mom said.

The trail turns and wends along the Multnomah Channel of the Willamette River. In 12 miles, at the tip of our island, it flows into the broad Columbia and then out to the Pacific. The twittering of wrens, sparrows, bushtits, juncos and chickadees resounds in the rainforest-like cacophony. Sixteen double-crested cormorants fly over the water, low to the surface. It pleases me to watch them fly free; in Asia, some cormorants are held captive with a small ring around the neck. They fish, but the ring prevents them from swallowing, and their catch is taken away by their keepers. Red and white berries decorate bare branches along the trail; the red are rose hips, transubstantiation of wild pink summer roses into winter sustenance for the woodland birds.

At Dad's side, we each sat and tried to quietly accept his gaspings. I could listen, but couldn't look, and hid behind first a newspaper, then a magazine. Who knows where consciousness ends? Mom, age 65, leaned over and whispered to me, "I've never watched anyone die before."

By four in the morning Dad had been calmed by drugs, his chest peacefully rising and lowering. Everyone went home but Mary Jane and I, who curled up in chairs, lulled to sleep by the rhythmic death rattling of Dad's breath.

Cro-o-ak. Cro-a-ak. Inch-long tree frogs in the marsh create a sound as gargantuan as an elephant's thump, their throat sacs bulging like inflated balloons. Why, I wonder, do we say something "croaked" when it dies? Frogs croak to attract a mate, leading to the creation of new life.

Through the airspace between tall Douglas-firs, two hawks sweep, spin and dive with dazzling acrobatics. Following them through my binoculars, the background becomes frosty white; focusing, I recognize Mount St. Helens, its flat-topped volcanic cone luminous with fresh snow—winter's blanket protecting budding trees and wildflowers that emerged from its ashes.

Day nine. With the respirator gone, Dad could be moved to a private room. Here, without the endless machines and digital readouts, without the tube in his mouth, the mask over his nose, this 70-year-old man who never went to a doctor finally looked peaceful. Within the hour, he stopped breathing.

Beneath gnarly-branched old oaks, galls decorate fallen leaves. They're at once beautiful and mysterious, these gold-brown mottled balls strangely connected to the leaf's surface. I gather a pocketful to take home for the mantle and accidentally break one. Thus cracked, its thin skin crumbles, revealing emptiness inside.

At the funeral Mass, our family sat in the first pew and I looked around the church. Through my eight years of grade school at St. Michael's, I'd gone to Mass in this church most every morning. Catholic high school. Catholic college. But I never felt spiritual in a church, even in the magnificent cathedrals of Europe—Notre Dame, St. Peters, the Duomo. They were simply human, marvels of architecture and artistry.

This church, especially. Its golden-winged angels and ornate pulpit of my youth had been replaced by bland oak furniture. Because of declining attendance, the six Catholic churches of Braddock had been merged into this one, renamed Good Shepherd. I looked around and felt not spirituality, but the brunt of priestly politics. All the statues from the old churches, which devout Babas and Zedos had prayed to every day of their lives, had been sold at an auction.

Now two weeks later, in this cathedral of tall trees, I allow my tears to flow unchecked, my sobs another sound in nature's litany. It's here that life feels sacred, amid the harmony of the bird-song choir. Amid the mystery of creation so alive in the inexpressible beauty of a wood duck feather, the unfathomable fire within the mountain. It's here that death feels natural, and I find peace: for unto dust thou shalt return.

Back at the front porch, I wipe the caked mud from my boots and notice a single rosebud ready to bloom.

PART 2
COURAGE

Chapter 6
Teed Off

"This is as beautiful as any place on earth," I remember thinking at the precise moment I fell in love with Sauvie Island. It was in 1984, during my first winter in Portland, on a gloriously unseasonable 70-degree January Sunday. Encircled by azure sky, the ring of Cascade mountains glistening with heavy snow, oak trees reflected in still waters, tundra swans winging overhead, I floated in my kayak intoxicated by the magnificence of it all.

In the fall of 1988, after Bob and I moved to the island and settled in, I realized it was the first place I'd ever lived where I wanted to stay.

Oregon has strong land use laws, so it did not seem foolish to trust that Sauvie's wild and pastoral panoramas would continue to be conserved. In most places, farmland like Sauvie's, ten miles from a major metropolitan area and surrounded by river shorelines, would have long ago been transformed into suburbia. But in 1977 Oregon passed farsighted land use laws to protect farms and forests. Prime farmlands are zoned EFU, or Exclusive Farm Use, and cannot be subdivided by more than one house on 76 acres. In practice it works well, maintaining large parcels of significant farmland. But a turn of events revealed that the law has an unseemly quirk: EFU lands be granted a Conditional Use permit—for a church, a school, a campground, or a golf course.

39

It is only our fifth month of living on Sauvie and the cocoon of nature's bliss is shattered by a small newspaper article headlined, "Golf course planned on Sauvie Island." It describes how a Japanese financial company has purchased 140 acres and optioned 60 more on the island, planning to build an 18-hole golf course plus "the usual amenities such a clubhouse and pro shop." This course won't be hidden away in some back areas, it will be the first panorama seen cresting the bridge. A timeless landscape of woods, fields and mountains that I've already come to treasure with each coming home will be developed into a manicured slice of suburbia. The thought of it turns my stomach into a knot.

In a panic I send a copy of the article to Jack Sanders, a savvy friend who's lived on and around the island for years. I write a note at the bottom, "A nightmare unfolds! Think there's anything that can be done now?" When he calls he goads me, "There's going to be a public hearing in a few weeks before the Planning Commission. I'm going to testify. You should, too."

"I've never done anything like that," I protest, uncomfortable with the idea. "I've never even *been* to a public hearing. I have no idea of what a Planning Commission is all about. I wouldn't know what to say."

"Say you're a landowner and you're opposed. This golf course issue has been around since '83. Why don't you and Bob come over for a beer and I'll tell you all about it."

A few days later we drop by and Jack recounts the story: In 1983, the farmer selling the land was granted a Conditional Use permit for a 125-acre golf course. Jack and a few others opposed it and lost. But the county commissioners put a gaggle of restrictions on the course to keep it a small, rural scale. The restaurant, for example, could have no more than 1,500 square feet of seating, and the proposed tennis courts were eliminated. Eventually the developer pulled out. Now the farmer wants to expand the permit to 200 acres for a tournament-size course. The Japanese developers must have big plans for it—they've hired one of the most famous golf course designers in the world.

Jack scoffs at the rationale: "The permit application says they need the extra acres for safety reasons—diminishing potential injury to golfers from stray golf balls."

"I'm just horrified that if this golf course goes in, it'll be the beginning of the end for the island as we know it today," I commiserate.

"Yeah, what's next?" Jack quips. "Pumpkin Patch Mall?"

To speak at a public hearing—the notion gnaws at me. For years I've donated money to conservation organizations, marched in rallies, switched lights off when I left a room, but never have I personally and individually stood up for the environment. Should I go and testify? What good would it do? It sounds as though the permit is already approved. Even if I help convince the commission not to allow the expansion, the developers still have approval to build a smaller course. What would I say? I have nothing tangible to fight with. I don't know the lingo of the Planning Commission. I'm afraid of sounding stupid. The excuses line themselves up, but in the end they have no strength. To speak at *this* public hearing—this is something I cannot not do.

Bob has the flu the evening of the Planning Commission hearing, so I drive into town with Jack, his thick graying hair and matching moustache almost aglow each time we pass beneath a street light. We park and walk briskly to the Multnomah County Courthouse, a staid old building with wide marble stairs leading up to the modern wood-paneled hearing room. Inside, the Planning Department's Staff Report is available and I'm disheartened when I read that it recommends approval.

The commission chairman announces that people who wish to testify should come forward, one at a time, and speak at the podium facing the commissioners. When a few other people argue against the expansion I'm somewhat encouraged. One man creates the harrowing scene of a dying child trapped in an ambulance stuck in tournament traffic. Another speaks of pesticides and archeology. Someone else uncovered traffic statistics and reports them. Jack talks of property values.

I say this:

> I am a homeowner on Sauvie Island and I would like
> to testify against this expansion.

A golf course—period—is totally out of keeping with the character of the island, which is: farmland, some residences, and recreation on land essentially in its natural state.

Only 435 families are listed in the island phone book. And we're to have a parking lot with 190 cars.

Land is zoned so 76 acres are a single-family dwelling. In spaces where two families might live, we'll have a parking lot with 190 cars.

So I testify against this expansion, to minimize as much as possible the denigration of this island that is my home—and as it exists, such a unique place for the people of this city and this county.

With negligible discussion, the Planning Commission approves the expansion. Jack and I, both depressed, don't say much on the drive home. I found the courage to speak up, but it seems not to have mattered, as though the decision was made before the hearing and nothing anyone said would have changed it. I felt unheard.

Two weeks later Bob and I walk through a gentle March rain to Carolyn Lee's houseboat. Inside, shaking out our jackets, we're introduced to others who'd testified at the hearing. Jerome DeGraaff, an Amsterdam-born university librarian, found everyone's addresses and brought us together to file an appeal. We're an inexperienced lot, in terms of land use issues. Besides Jack and Bob, both video producers, Carolyn is an art gallery manager and former dancer. Jeanne Bevis is a counselor, and her husband, Stu Sandler, an engineer and writer.

Strong hot coffee in hand, snugly seated in her grandmother's navy velvet sofa in front of the wood-burning stove, I listen as Jerome explains the situation. "The Planning Commission approved the expansion. But we can appeal to a higher authority, the Board of County Commissioners, who have the power to overturn the decision.

It costs $535 to file the appeal. $150 is the filing fee, which we have to pay right away. $385 is to transcribe the hearing tapes, but there was a problem when the tapes were made. I'm told they're not transcribable. Which means not only would we save the $385, but the law entitles us to a whole new hearing, called a *de novo* hearing."

Stu adds, "I called 1000 Friends of Oregon, which as you probably know, is a land-use watchdog group. They think we have a strong case, for one thing, because the only traffic study is six years old. They also mentioned that the archeological report is superficial, and the permit file has a letter from the state Department of Fish and Wildlife pointing out that the landowner is significantly changing land use and locating in an area identified as significant wildlife habitat and the Department won't be responsible for responding to any wildlife damage that occurs—so there aren't any provisions to protect wildlife. They advise us to get a lawyer."

"Okay, let's get busy," Jack urges. "Here's the form we need to fill out. What are our 'Grounds for Reversal of Decision?'"

We haggle impassionately for more than an hour and decide to list seven points: expanded tournament impact, insufficient traffic data, inadequate provisions for wildlife, lack of application continuity, pesticides, superficial archeology survey, and vagueness of boundaries. This last refers to the fact that even though the farmer's Conditional Use permit was for 125 acres, he's claiming the land approved is 145 acres. We each pitch in $25 and request a *de novo* hearing.

By the second meeting we seem like old friends, innately connected by our cause, munching on a potluck of pizza, curried rice and Tuscan bread. This time Dave Kunkel, the lanky young man in blue jeans who testified about traffic, joins our group. He's a partner in Columbia Farms, at 3,000 acres the largest agricultural operation on the island. And he's found something very interesting.

"There's a letter in the file in the Planning Department from 1985," Dave begins, "where an attorney says that the Conditional Use permit should be renewed—and it was—because the farmer has done substantial development and construction toward the golf course. But the things he mentions—applying herbicides, removing spoil from drainage ditches, deep tilling—that's just basic farming stuff. And one thing—about gravelling and grading the golf course access road—I'm sure he's talking about his brother's driveway."

"Would you be willing to get up and say that at the appeals hearing?" Jack asks. "It might make you pretty unpopular with some of the other farmers who'd like to sell out, too."

Dave rubs his chin. "I'd do it."

Jerome, Stu and I are seated in the county hearing room in a state of frenzy. This morning the Board of County Commissioners, who have accepted our appeal, will determine its scope—that is, whether they will hear arguments on all seven of our issues. We found an attorney to help us, Betsy Newcomb, who lives a few miles down the road from me. Yesterday our item was listed last on the agenda, but now it's been moved to first, and Betsy's not here yet.

We feel helpless as we are told that the hearing tapes were sent to an audio studio for augmentation, and are now deemed transcribable. Thus, the scope would be limited to what's already on the record, with new information allowed only regarding traffic. We have no idea what to do.

When Betsy arrives at the appointed time, it's all over. We explain what happened and, with six weeks to go before our appeals hearing, she says simply, "We have a lot of work to do."

The following day Stu gets a letter from the planning director saying "the exact amount of the appeal fee has now been determined to be $535.00. You have ten days from today to pay the required transcript fee of $385.00. Failure to comply shall preclude review by the Board."

We scrape together the money, and within a few weeks, we've distributed more than a thousand flyers, mailed to friends, passed out at meetings, posted at outdoors stores, even at my hairdresser's. Jeanne has chosen to work on these things behind the scenes, not wanting to rattle her close relationship with her aunt, who's owned an island farm since the '40s and is a long-time friend of the farmer. We've begun a letter-writing campaign to the county commissioners. Our writeups were published in various newsletters. We opened a post office box, a checking account, and decided to call ourselves the Sauvie Island Conservancy.

Salad bowls and platters of pasta squeeze between stacks of research at our weekly potlucks. We fill flip charts, storm in outrage, play devil's advocate and divvy up assignments. One week I'm assigned the task of finding out more about tournament golf courses.

A long day in the main library poring through years of golf, business and environmental magazines turns up a single but powerful gem: the designer for the course invented "stadium golf," and his tournament courses are designed for 50,000 to 60,000 spectators. When I come home, I phone the office of the Portland Trailblazers, our professional basketball team. All home games are sellouts, capacity, 13,000. I think about the quagmire of cars stuck in traffic after their games and count the number of streets and freeway lanes leaving the Coliseum. There are 17. How many lanes leave Sauvie Island? One.

Spaced around the conference table in the bustling offices of 1000 Friends of Oregon, Betsy, Stu, Jerome and I overload busy senior planner Paul Ketcham with our story. He's squeezed some time for us between two meetings.

"You've got them beat right here," Paul says, opening a large notebook of state laws almost immediately to the correct page. "Here it is: a Conditional Use permit expires in two years without substantial construction, development or use. This makes a mockery of that standard. And if there's no substantial construction, you can argue that the permit should have expired and they need to make a new application for a golf course.

"Here's something else, about that 145 acres. When the county commissioners approved the course in 1983, as a governing body, they *understood* that they were approving only 125 acres. The applicant can't come back now and say that because the metes and bounds total 145 acres, the commissioners approved that.

"Also, you've got some other strategies: The road systems aren't adequate. Appeal to the commissioners' long-range vision of planning. Check on how many other golf courses are being built in the area. Is there a need? But I think, most important, they definitely haven't met the standard of substantial construction. The permit is clearly invalid."

He looks at his watch. "I hope that helps. I'm due in another meeting."

Passing around trays of pancakes slathered in fresh island strawberries and syrup, we try to focus our research.

Jerome has reams of data about chemicals. "The pesticides golf courses use are horrendous. Insecticides, fungicides, herbicides. Triple, quadruple what farmers use. Not only that, they're applied continuously, year round. I found one article where a golfer died from an allergic reaction to a chemical sprayed weekly on his country club golf course."

"I spoke with a wildlife biologist from the U.S. Department of Agriculture," Carolyn says. "He wrote a letter to the commissioners saying 'The sheer numbers of geese the golf course will attract will be alarming. It appears that the developer is under the assumption that several methods of dispersing geese exist. This is not the case. One method for hazing geese for golf courses is a combination of shooting pyrotechnics and actual harassment, or chasing.'

"Then I found something even better. This is a quote from the farmer that was in *The Oregonian*." She reads, "He said if the geese and ducks become a problem, he would spray the damaged areas with a product that temporarily makes the birds sick."

Dave adds, "Then we've got this article about the moratorium on golf courses on farmlands in Honolulu. It tells how golf courses have drastically raised property values and taxes, driving farmers out of business."

Bob has been collecting articles attacking us. He reads from a letter the farmer and his wife wrote in our island newsletter. "Dear Friends and Neighbors …We are writing to clarify any questions that some of you may have concerning our original intent for the public golf course proposal…As usual, people who do not live in our area, nor share our local concerns and taxes, are *once again* trying to dictate the usage of property on the island."

Betsy is troubled. "We've got to find a way to open the hearing to these other issues. As it stands, we're only permitted to present information about traffic. And we could use more time to develop our arguments. For example, we seem to have forgotten that they're basing this whole expansion on the issue of safety. We haven't even begun to look into that."

Jack interjects, "Donna and I are going to send out press releases this week. Has everybody reviewed our copy?"

KINK radio calls first. Can they send a reporter out to interview me? The following day I listen to myself on the morning news. Then Tom McAllister calls from *The Oregonian* and two days before the hearing I'm quoted in his column. Jerome is on television, KATU-TV. With a backdrop of flocks of waterfowl lifting off, reporter Al Sigala says, "Not everybody is happy with the idea of putting a golf course here. On the northern end of the island is a wildlife refuge. Hundreds of thousands of waterfowl stop here during the migration season. And although the golf course would be located on the other side of the island, there is still concern."

While I am pleased by the self-garnered publicity, I'm saddened by it as well, for it comes with a loss. When Bob and I moved to the island, I imagined myself joining the Grange and hearing the stories of old-timers, people whose family names still grace the island roads. But the Grange officially supports the farmer, even though many of its members don't want to see the island developed. Some long-time residents will come up to me and tell me personally they believe in what we're doing, but make excuses, "Oh, my wife is a friend of the farmer's wife, so I can't say anything." They have anonymously given us money. But because they won't come publicly forward, I become the pariah. This is not what I would have chosen for myself. I think about it constantly, but know that whatever the outcome, I could do no less.

Inside the county Board Room the day of the hearing, the far wall is lined with television cameras, and newspaper, television and radio reporters. The publicity guarantees that, at the very least, the county commissioners can't ignore what we have to say.

Betsy immediately charges that the Conditional Use permit should have expired. She reiterates the discrepancies between the 125 and the 145 acres. Then she turns to the actual transcripts, pointing out that there are more than 240 inaudible remarks in 90 pages. In some places entire statements are missing. One page alone has 13 blanks. Some of our own testimonies were transcribed incorrectly. How can the county commissioners make a fair decision? Betsy asks. She requests some latitude in determining what, exactly, is "on the record."

Under the glaring television lights, commissioner Pauline Anderson readily admits that she couldn't follow the transcript. Others concur. Without much deliberation, we're awarded a full new hearing, to be held in four weeks.

Reporters crowd around and I somehow become the spokesperson. I think I speak well, but watching myself on television that night, I see that my nervousness made me fast-talking and strident. I feel I've embarrassed us all. I'm nicely quoted, though, in the next day's newspaper. The article proclaims our small victory, announcing that "the new hearing will allow 45 minutes of unrestricted testimony after a conservation group requested that more testimony be allowed at the hearing." It ends with "[the farmer] said that if the expansion is denied, he will petition to the Land Use Board of Appeals."

"If the expansion is denied?"

We're as surprised as anyone that we're recognized as "a conservation group" and a force to be reckoned with.

Chapter 7
The Purple Martin Man

Perched atop a 20-foot ladder embedded in river mud and lashed to a piling, Dave Fouts grasps the cold aluminum with one hand, and with the other, forcefully swings a hammer. It's Saturday, March 14, 1992. Blam! Off comes a roof. Blam! Blam! One wall. Then another. With a final whack, the last of the old purple martin house breaks away and lands in the paint-peeled boat below, making way for a new one.

"Say, do you know anyone who can come out and help me this weekend?" Dave had asked Thursday afternoon. "I'm going to put up more martin houses along the channel."

"What kind of help do you need?"

"Just someone to keep an eye on me, really, in case I get in trouble."

No kidding. At the last piling he couldn't reach the houses and was tempted to set the ladder in the boat and climb from there. Reflected wakes from speeding powerboats made that too dangerous so he relented, not ungrudgingly, because that meant two fewer homes for the martins this year.

Purple martins are the largest American swallow, glossy blue-black songbirds that have been disappearing from the Northwest since the 1940s. For millennia, they have built their nests in cavities in snags of ancient trees. Old-timers remember the martin as a common bird.

But snags rotted away, or were destroyed with clearcutting, and the martins took to nesting in cavities of river pilings and sometimes, cornices of Victorian houses. Dave contends that the purple martin was one of the first species impacted by clearcuts, long before anyone noticed the decline of the northern spotted owl. Then in 1946 a strong competitor arrived, the starling, ousting purple martins from the remaining holes. By 1965 the starling population had exploded, and martins, along with western bluebirds, had nearly vanished from British Columbia down through California.

By the mid-1980s, only 20 pair nested along this Multnomah Channel of the Willamette River. Last summer, thanks to Dave's almost single-handed efforts, there were nearly 100. About 250 pair currently nest in a dozen or so colonies in the Portland-Vancouver region; 2,000 would be considered a healthy population.

Dave, a bear-sized man with graying hair and piercing blue eyes, gracefully backs down the extension ladder and reaches into the boat, filling his pocket with nails from a small paper bag. Back up the ladder, he pounds the nails in place with one hand, then comes down to retrieve a new martin house, which he sets in position on the nails, then hammers in place. The houses are numbered; this one is 78. It's with these designations that Dave keeps track of the martins' nesting success.

The 10- x 6-inch houses are his own adaptation, very different from traditional martin "apartments" in the east and midwest. *Progne subis arboricola* is Oregon's subspecies of purple martin—"tree-dweller" by definition. These western martins are larger birds.

The house's entrance hole is exactly the right millimeter for martins, a deterrent for nest-invading starlings. "Starlings can actually squeeze their way in," Dave admits, then adds with a devilish grin, "But they have a hell of a time getting out!"

Caulked and sealed, the houses offer a warm, dry apartment and nursery. And there's even a little porch, with roughened wood so the new babies can get a good grip and not fall off.

"What's that?" I ask, as he attaches a string with a wooden block to the house.

"It's a plug, to keep out other birds," he explains. Violet green and tree swallows abound on the island and would take up residence in the houses before the martins arrive. Dave pulls out the plugs when the martins return, using a long pole. This house is barely nailed to the piling and a tree swallow dips and dives around it, eyeing for an entrance.

A 40-foot power boat screams by, its wake breaking against the mud-held ladder and crashing against the shoreline. The ladder has been slowly sinking, and now Dave comes down to extend it farther, straddling the boat and ladder rung.

I met Dave three years ago, the first time I attended the Oregon Department of Fish and Wildlife's annual planning meeting for the Sauvie Island Wildlife Area. His brash outspokenness in the face of a roomful of hunters and hunting dog trainers lent me courage. "This place has been sort of a big hunting club," he said by way of explanation. "No one was supporting biodiversity."

"I have a highly visible project for a Sensitive species, and quite often I feel *persona non grata* on the wildlife area. It took practically an Act of Congress to get in some areas, but traditional groups, like the dog trials, have *carte blanche* to do what they want.

"Oh, yes, I get a lot of angry stares from people, including ODFW staff, but somebody's got to speak up. Sauvie Island should be for all wildlife. That it isn't really angers me."

Dave became intrigued with purple martins when he was 11 years old, walking along a lakeshore in southern Michigan. "It was just love at first sight," he beams. "There was something unique about them. They're brilliant purple, with a real pretty call, hard to describe, a kind of *chooo, chooo, chooo.* I was just enchanted with them."

Immediately he started pressing his mother for a purple martin house. Although he never established a colony, "enough came around to really spur my interest." When was 16, his family moved back to Portland; Dave was disappointed to leave the martins behind, but his life was filled with other things.

Seventeen years later he was trying out a new camera, photographing the recently-erupted Mount St. Helens, when he heard something familiar. Sure enough—purple martins. They'd found nesting holes in the old pilings of a long-dismantled sawmill.

For the next five years, he spent a lot of time sitting and watching the birds as he fished near a spot on the northern tip of Sauvie Island.

But when ODFW allowed crayfish to be commercially harvested

there, the fishing fell off dramatically. "I loved coming out to the place. I'd been a consumptive user of wildlife all these years, and I wanted to do something for the environment." Around that time, the U.S. Fish and Wildlife Service came out with a report on west coast purple martins that painted a dismal picture. And so Dave's purple martin project was born.

"In the beginning, the minute I put a nest up, it would be almost immediately occupied, they were so desperate."

Through fall and winter he spends hundreds of hours, and his own money, building nest boxes, and sanding, painting and drilling holes in Calabash gourds. One purple martin devours more than a thousand insects a day, and Native Americans placed gourds in their villages because the martins chased crows away from crops. Dave thinks in some ways gourds are more effective, since their swaying scares off starlings and sparrows, but they're more labor-intensive, since they need to be brought indoors and kept dry over the winter. He has only a few dozen gourds in place, but more than a hundred homes.

"It's just like having another job," he says, on top of his full-time work as a respiratory therapist at the Veterans Affairs Medical Center.

In the spring, he travels up and down the Columbia, across the island's Wildlife Area and up and down Multnomah Channel, removing and replacing weathered, leaky old houses. Gourds are re-suspended.

Then he waits.

It's believed the martins migrate from wintering grounds in South America. Scouts arrive mid-April, followed by the first wave of adults later that month, and a second wave in mid-May. Sub adults start arriving the first of June.

Dave releases the plugs. Then watches.

Like an anxious parent, he grouses about how the martins will spend a month "gadding about from place to place, fooling around. This hurts them. They'll spend a whole day away, and sometimes starlings will take over that area." He frets about house sparrows, too. "Those nasty, vicious, little creatures."

Eventually, the metallic-blue birds will settle down. It take about two weeks for the eggs to hatch and about another month until the babies are well-feathered, ready to fledge. "You should hear them," Dave laughs. "The parents can never feed them enough. They're increasingly vocal about their wants. I love to go out and watch them."

He's noticed that when the chicks are small, the parents bring them smaller insects, then progressively larger ones. When the babies are ready to fledge, they're eating a diet largely of dragonflies. Once the young fledge, the parents begin taking the chicks around with them, and by late August, with the adults leading the babies, they head south. Purple martins are one of the last species to arrive in the spring, and one of the first to leave.

Throughout the nesting season, Dave conducts inventories of the breeding pairs, with yearly records of each bird. Last year's was very successful, and he exults, "I'm looking for a lot of little purple birds this year."

For now he's finished, a total of four replacement houses and four new ones. Collapsing the ladder, he positions it in the boat and sputters off along the pilings toward the old ferry dock.

In another few weeks Dave will be out here daily, waiting for flashes of purple and listening for the sounds of a soft *chooo, chooo, chooo* in the evening air.

Chapter 8
Of Habits and Habitat

Jim Charlton, of Charlton Kennels, of Charlton's Duck Club, of Charlton Road, of the Charlton family that's lived on the island since the Civil War, is seated next to me at the planning table. The choice was neither of ours.

I'd met the man only once, at an island meeting on August 28, 1991 led by the Oregon Department of Fish and Wildlife. About 70 people showed up, each with a biased interest in the future management of Sauvie's Wildlife Area. By my count, there were ten or so ODFW officials, a dozen and a half island residents, 40 hunters and hunting dog trainers, and three environmentalists. We label each other this way, often with disdain, and it is our habit to position ourselves as adversaries.

The officials divided us into a quartet of groups and told us to list priorities for the new ten-year Wildlife Area Management Plan. With trepidation but conviction I'd raised my hand and said, "Access for wildlife watchers during hunting season." A tall, plaid-shirted man with a graying moustache and wire-rim glasses railed in disgust. "I can see it coming! Before you know it, they'll be wanting to get rid of all the hunting on the island. Mark my words." I looked away without responding, knowing that I'd be invited to the planning table, where it counted.

Now, this man's name card has been set next to mine. He turns and asks, "What year's your 911?" I'd seen him watch me maneuver out of my funky orange Porsche. "1970," I answer. "It's quite a bomb." He takes this in. "Good-looking car, though."

Along a hedgerow thick with blackberry bushes, Greg Baker's Intermediate Birdwatching class listens for the whistle of a golden-crowned sparrow. He imitates the three descending notes. "It sounds like Oh, dear, me, Oh, dear, me. Do you hear that?" A week later we would not be permitted to gather at this same spot; like most of the Wildlife Area's 12,000 acres, it will be closed to public during the three-month hunting season. As we discuss the upcoming closure, most of the group is indignant. I explain: No, the money to manage Sauvie's Wildlife Area doesn't come from state taxes. Yes, I used to think that, too. But no, it comes from hunting and fishing dollars. No, from licenses, stamps and a tax on firearms and ammunition. No, this land was purchased beginning in the late '40s with funding from the Pittman-Robertson Act, hunters' money. Yes, all this land was bought and managed for nearly half a century with hunting and fishing money.

It's been called "environmentalism's dirty little secret." Everywhere hunters wield their weapons on state wildlife lands, though the copses of New England, southern swamps, ice-held lakes of the north, midwest woodlands, moss-clinging rainforests of the Pacific Northwest, the story is the same. Much habitat has been preserved—not by environmental groups—but by those who desired to protect habitat for the hunt, as well as other gun owners. Through the Pittman-Robertson Act, by 1991 over $2 billion had been raised and 4,000,000 acres purchased for wildlife. When hunters act like they own these lands, they don't. But they did contribute to buying them.

So habitats were purchased, but for what protection, at what expense? Hunted species like deer, alligators, black bears and wild turkeys are thriving to the point where in some places they are considered pests, yet other species are dissipating to extinction. In Oregon, the numbers of Canada geese are on the increase, the birds swarming like locusts to decimate newly-planted farm fields, while over 150 other wildlife species are listed as Sensitive or Threatened and Endangered. Even the state bird, the western meadowlark, has nearly vanished from the western half of the state.

And so I sit at the planning table in the church basement next to Jim Charlton, surrounded by representatives from the Oregon Duckhunters Association, the Oregon Retrievers Trial Club, Oregon Ducks Unlimited. Jim Charlton represents the Oregon Landowners and Waterfowlers. We have been invited to help revise Sauvie Island Wildlife Area's ten-year plan through a process known as the CRMP, Coordinated Resource Management Plan. Across the table is Marc Liverman from Portland Audubon, and Roy Elicker from the National Wildlife Federation. As environmentalists we have no clout, since people who hunt and fish are ODFW's paying clientele. What we do have is directive Number Two of the new state wildlife area recommendations: "Goals and objectives should be specific and measurable, with a greater emphasis on *all* wildlife species." During our monthly all-day meetings, three so far, we inch through the old plan, niggling over each word, the work painfully stagnant.

"Okay, is it agreed that we'll remove the sentence that says 'Red clover has been planted since 1987 as a green forage crop for geese. See page 4a for additional information?'"

"We're going to leave in the sentence, 'In the 1970s mounds were tried but erosion washed them out, any future mounds would need riprap to stabilize.' And we're going to add 'and platforms' after 'mounds.'"

"Two paragraphs down we're going to change 'Current nest-box program for wood ducks will be maintained. A new design of boxes using native materials will be tested with intention of greatly expanding the program. Nesting trees will be maintained.' This will be replaced with 'Current nest box programs and trees for cavity will be maintained and increased where feasible using volunteers where possible.'"

We've been dancing around the real issues, the reasons most of us have given our days to this: Should there be more grazing, to create low grass to lure Canada geese? Or less grazing, to reduce the cow trampling and manure, especially around lakes, bird nesting areas and riparian zones? Should dog trials and training continue to be permitted? Do such traditional uses outweigh environmental concerns about disturbances to wildlife? Should the old plan be rubber-stamped, as some would like? Or revised to manage the habitat for wildlife diversity and protect all Sensitive species?

I have a difficult time at these meetings, not just because they're interminably tedious, bellicose and badly managed. It's that I'm not true to myself. For more years than I can recall, I've been an ethical vegetarian, a dozen times a day abiding by a spiritual belief not to kill animals for food. But at these meetings I represent the Sauvie Island Conservancy, whose members have agreed to remain neutral on the issue of hunting.

I look around the table, slowly, and listen to the language of wildlife management—game, resources, sport, the harvest—and wonder how each person translates those euphemisms into life and death, animal spirits and bird souls.

After seven contentious all-days meetings at the planning table, the groups surprises itself one morning in a unanimous voice. ODFW, without telling any of our CRMP group, has bulldozed a lake shore in the wildlife area and begun a $94,000 development. Everyone is outraged by the deception, and unquelled by the agency's protest that this was based on an already-approved plan other than the one we're writing.

Suddenly one environmentalist, who all along had been advocating for a reduction in cow grazing, pronounces that "grazing cows would have less impact than a 100-car parking lot!"

A hunter who never before appeared to care about any species other than waterfowl bellows, "You bulldozed a boat ramp right where you said those Sensitive species of western pond turtles are living!"

Jim Charlton says, "I think in good faith to us you need to stop construction right now."

I add, "I agree with Jim. But I also ask that you go one step further and actually remove that boat ramp."

Around the table there are grudging nods of agreement. A few weeks later Dave Kunkel phones to say he'd been at an island meeting where people were attacking me. "I stood up for you," he lets me know, and adds, "Jim Charlton did, too. He said he doesn't always agree with you, but he respects you."

More than a year passes, and with it 14 all-day meetings at the planning table. That's nearly three work-weeks of time for each of us, who are bonded now by perseverance if nothing else. Most of us have given up on the process and individually or in small groups hounded the agency's director. In my letter, I pointed out that this new version in-progress doesn't meet the state's guidelines because there's not a single specific and measurable goal or objective. And, among other things, there is no protection for Sensitive or Threatened and Endangered species. I had been one of 60 people from around the state whom ODFW invited to a two-day "Second Century Summit" to develop a "strategic plan for the next century" that was supposed to add "increased emphasis on the sustainability, restoration and enhancement of fish and wildlife habitat." I commented to the director that "The Second Century is happening right now... but unfortunately, it's looking exactly like the First." ODFW, wearied of our squabbling, has decided to take our comments and have a staff person write the new plan.

After sundry revisions, the new ten-year Sauvie Island Wildlife Area Management Plan is presented for approval before the state Fish and Wildlife Commission in Salem. Representatives from the CRMP testify to air our concerns one final time. While many from the group reject the proposal, I and Michael Carlson, who has replaced Marc Liverman for Portland Audubon, come forward to give it a nod, even though we both have concerns about it.

My testimony supports the plan, and I recognize that there are important changes within. There's been a shift to "overall habitat considerations." The plan "recognizes the needs of all wildlife species." Foot travel is encouraged, roads in the backcountry will be closed, open fires will be prohibited, and grazing significantly decreased. However, the plan doesn't come close to creating specific and measurable goals. There's no substantive data on wildlife except for "game" waterfowl. The new plan arbitrarily closes most wildlife areas to the public for six months, instead of three. The number of hunting dog trials was not reduced. And there is nothing specific to prevent more recreational development. But even with these problems, which are serious, I speak for the Conservancy in recommending approval of the plan. It's a long way from where it should be, but a long way from where it's been.

A few weeks later there's a message on my phone machine from Jim Charlton. "I'd like to invite you to come and see my place. Friday morning looks good." I want Bob to come, so I call Jim and arrange that we'll be out Saturday morning. "Be here by eight," Jim advises, "The birds are gone by 9:30."

We drive the quarter mile down a dirt road back to the Charlton Kennels. Getting out of the car, we're aware of a tremendous sound of geese emerging from a distant fog. The kennels are sited along the Gilbert River, with a two-person bench along the water, a tube bird feeder alongside in a tree and another next to the building. Jim comes right out and we walk through the mud across a field. "There's a ghost fog this morning," he says. "See any Indian ghosts?"

"Do you see Indian ghosts?" I ask.

He says in almost a whisper, "Sometimes you feel like you're not alone out here."

Jim estimates that on a given day he's feeding 2,000 waterfowl. Twice he's gone at his own expense to the Pacific Flyway Conference. He explains, "The numbers of geese are increasing every year. Public lands make up only about five percent of the waterfowl feeding areas. The other 95 percent is done by private owners like me." We walk to the rows of corn planted for feed. Yesterday they mowed a few rows and today the corn on most of the cobs in half gone.

About six-foot-four and slim, he speaks assertively, his face surprisingly unweathered for all the time he spends outdoors tending his 200 acres and training dogs. We come to a lake he created, with islands within. "There's only one strip of land to get in or out," he shows. "That keeps predators like coyotes off there for the most part." Pointing to depressions on the lake bottom, he describes the nutgrass that he's seeded. Waterfowl dig for the nuts at the roots of the grasses. An immature bald eagle flies overhead.

After an hour encircling the land, startling thousands of Canada geese, tundra swans, pintails, mallards and widgeon, Jim looks me directly in the eye and says, "I just wanted you to see what we have here. I really appreciate the wildlife. Hunters in our club took 114 birds this year. A disease in one season in just one area of the flyway can wipe out more birds than all the hunters. If you looked at how much money we spend in crops, well, I'm not making much money on hunting. We kill some birds, but you can see we give back much more than we take."

"I can see that," I say, as hundreds of geese thunder off behind.

Chapter 9
F.A.U.N.A.

A revival meeting, that's what it's like! A thigh-slapping, arms-flailing, spirit-rocking revival meeting! Gospel of the Evangelical Environmentalists. More than 250 of the Faithful, the region's most ardent grassroots conservationists, are gathered on a stormy night, January 10, 1990, at Houck's invitation, to form a coalition called Friends and Advocates of Urban Natural Areas—F.A.U.NA.

I hadn't intended to go at all, but the weather was so horrendous earlier when I talked to Mike he was afraid no one would show up. He was especially concerned because he had invited Neal Peirce to be guest speaker. Peirce, a Washington, D.C. syndicated columnist in town for an urban growth planning conference, would speak about similar efforts in other parts of the country. So I steered my 20-year-old car, a headlight out again, through the raven-black bleak night. After the formal presentations, Mike takes the podium. "I recognize a lot of people in the audience from small grassroots organizations. I know who you are, because I've worked with you. But you don't know each other. So how about if we go around the room and you can mention what your group is doing." The fires are unleashed. From the back, the front, the second row, the 15th row, the standing-room-only aisles, voice after voice booms out:

"We're fighting wetland fills!"

"We're trying to stop developers from building 1,400 houses along our creek!"

"We're the people who saved the Corbett Street Oak!"

"We're trying to halt road construction in our canyon!"

"We're training volunteers to monitor our polluted lake!"

"We've organized a coalition to stop construction of a dam!"

And, of course, me, "We're the ones fighting the multimillion dollar golf course on Sauvie Island!"

Bursts of applause resound after each outpouring. Amen! Amen! Amen! Most of us have been working within the vacuum of our small, geographically-focused conservation groups. We realize with joy that we've found, at last, a large and exuberant congregation of kindred souls.

On the phone one day, Mike offhandedly mentions that F.A.U.N.A. will produce a directory of all the grassroots organizations, which he estimates at 25 to 30. Immediately I see the value. No more bicycling to the parking lot and sticking flyers on people's windshields. No more blindly mailing flyers to friends. We'll know whom to call, who will act, who will have research on hand. I've done enough work to know what information will be useful.

Like a stream overflowing its banks, I gush with ideas: "What are you going to include in it? It needs a lot more than just name, address, contact person and phone number. I'd like to know about each group: How many members? Do you have meetings? How often? Do you have a newsletter? When is it published? Can we speak about our issue at your meetings? Can we distribute handouts? Could we include an article in your newsletter? Or a one-page flyer?"

"Hold on!" Mike laughs. "Come to our next Steering Committee meeting. I'm sure your input will be appreciated."

F.A.U.N.A.'s board meetings are held in the conference room of Murase Associates, landscape architects. More significantly, they're two floors above the microbrewery Bridgeport Brewpub, makers of Blue Heron beer and, in my opinion, the best pizza in town. In this atmosphere the periods are deemed superfluous and the coalition becomes simply FAUNA. Dave is one of the few people I know. As we go around the table introducing ourselves, he says, "Dave Fouts. Friends of Purple Martins." Mike slams his hand on the table.

"Dave, that's great! I've never heard you say that before. Friends of Purple Martins." Sheepishly, Dave allows, "It *is* only me." Mike says, "Yeah, but now you're official." The group moves through their ambitious agenda and when they begin to talk about the directory, Mike invites me to share my ideas. "If you're volunteering to do it, I'll help," Esther Lev offers. I gulp.

The directory never makes it to the top of the agenda, but I keep coming back to the Steering Committee meetings, now with 31 members. As the weather warms, we move downstairs to the brewpub, seated at tables outside on a loading dock. Mellow scents of hops and barley waft through the evening breeze. The alley between this building and the next is cobbled, zippered with a set of train tracks. An old bridge covered with ivy connects the second floors. The meetings might be finished in an hour or two, but we sit there till long past dark, drinking the rich, freshly-brewed beer and talking, about our travels, our families, our work. Many of the other board members are conservation professionals—wildlife biologists or people working for environmental organizations. This summer I've been writing an especially boring series of video training programs and ponder aloud if it isn't time for a career shift. But I can't see where there could be any position for me, with no science background, in the conservation movement.

In late July, Mike phones, "I think I might have a job for you. Let's meet for a beer." When we get together, he explains, "I have this grant from Meyer Memorial Trust. Part of the funding should be used to get FAUNA organized, and the way things are going I think I need to hire someone to give it a jump start. Are you interested?" Interested? I could not be more elated.

We agree on a three-month part-time contract, and Mike pulls out a list under the heading of "TASKS," handwritten with a fat red marker. I would produce the directory, write newsletters, develop a logo and letterhead, coordinate volunteers, answer phone inquiries, run the meetings, get out the minutes, and be FAUNA's spokesperson. It's almost exactly what I've been doing for the Sauvie Island Conservancy.

FAUNA needs a headquarters, and Bob Murase offers us a large unused back room with white walls, high ceilings and tall, paned windows—but no furniture. Annette Lalka finds out about a free used office furniture auction that a bank sponsors for non-profit organizations.

On a grey September Saturday, Annette and I are joined at the auction by two other board members, Mary Rose Navarro and Carol Pinegar. We've been lucky. Out of about 150 organizations, we're number five. Since ten groups make their choices at the same time, this means we get first pick. The auction resembles a relay race. One person from each of the ten groups goes to the "starting line" and gets five stick-ems with their number. When the organizer says "Go!" Annette passes out our stick-ems and we race to claim the pieces we want most: two conference tables, a legal-size file cabinet and two oak desks.

Mary Rose arranged for a friend with a borrowed pickup to meet us here and Annette joins them, making two trips to the office. Carol and I hang around to see if there are any leftover chairs, which can be claimed by anyone. They're abundant and we choose 11, squeezing them into her van. The door doesn't lock, though. It doesn't even close completely, so I twist around from the front seat, holding the door tight, envisioning it flying open and us chasing after our office chairs, swiveling and sliding down the highway. When we get to Murase's, all the other furniture's been brought up but the freight elevator is now stuck. We four women lug the heavy chairs up the building's three flights of creaking wooden steps. Finishing touches are added before the next meeting: wildlife and wetlands posters, and Dave's hanging purple martin gourds.

In assembling FAUNA's directory, I accumulate information on 56 groups around the region, about double what anyone had imagined. The organizations' local memberships total more than 22,000 people, an impressive number by any measure. In our rush to produce the directory in time for the October general membership meeting, Esther and I work late one night over a pot of tea, the pages emerging one by one from her ink jet printer. Jeanne Galick's illustration combining a heron in flight with a city background graces the cover. Our first printing is nearly gone within the month.

Part of the goal for establishing FAUNA was to create a powerful coalition to rally citizen support for the Regional Natural Areas Program, a project that Mike and others had been working on for a year and a half. A truly regional approach, that cuts across jurisdictional boundaries, is necessary to protect enough expanses of habitat to form a natural areas infrastructure, what Mike likes to call a *green-frastructure,* in our urban environment.

"The Regional Natural Areas Program?" I crinkle my nose in disdain and tease Mike. "That's a really ungainly title. I think it needs a jazzier name than that." "Well, then, come up with one," he challenges. So a FAUNA subcommittee is formed, a collective with decades of award-winning expertise in media communications, advertising, marketing and public relations. I've invited everyone to come to a half-day brainstorming session, and urged folks to scour books and other sources for meaningful words that evoke images of wild and natural green places teeming with wildlife, valuable for recreation and important as habitat.

I arrive at the gathering with a fondness for the word "greenspaces," which to me has a nice ring to it, and the feeling of a more all-encompassing version of the word *greenway* as popularized by Charles Little's book, *Greenways for America.* I've taken it step further and secretly have a proposed name, *Columbia Greenspaces,* for the major river threading through much of the region.

Flip chart at the ready, the group comes up with a multitude of words and names, and after much discussion, chooses the title *Metropolitan Greenspaces.* After much more discussion, we agree on a tag line, "A cooperative regional system of natural areas, open space, trails and greenways, for wildlife and people."

Next the committee goes back to the drawing board to come up with a logo. A designer will create the actual illustration, but the group ultimately agrees and suggests that it should feature a kingfisher, a common but not usually celebrated bird, with urban buildings in the background, and a woodcut style.

By early November FAUNA's premier newsletter is published. Introducing its feature article, "Saving the Pieces," which describes 21 regional projects and ballot initiatives to protect wildlife, Mike writes,

> It's easy to get discouraged when hearing the dire
> predictions of growth for our region. While it might
> seem tempting to pull up stakes and head over the
> next hill, sometimes the greener pastures are gone
> there, too. And they will be all gone, unless people are
> willing to do something about it. Fortunately, that's
> what's been happening all around our region.

The Metropolitan Greenspaces Program is featured on pages 7 and 8, officially introducing the proposal to FAUNA members. Under the heading of "Knitting the Pieces Together/The Big Picture," the story describes the program's four phases, ending with a greenspaces acquisition program.

The phone never stops. Through FAUNA, I have the pleasure of speaking at a Greenspaces Economics Conference with Dr. David Goode from the London Ecology Centre. I host a busload of politicians at my home for breakfast after a wildlife tour. I'm responsible for coordinating a Greenspaces exhibit at the Home & Garden Show attended by 65,000 people. Invited by the World Affairs Council, I speak to young German politicians, my stories translated through their headphones. The work seems to snowball, gathering speed at a dizzying rate. It's soon time for a second newsletter. Data base. Phone tree. Displays at the Salmon Festival and Friends of Trees conference. Garden Club slide show. Workshops: "How to Start a 'Friends' Group." "How to Speak at a Public Hearing." "How to Promote Your Group's Events." My three-month contract is extended indefinitely.

"Where is FAUNA going?" the Steering Committee continually asks. Mike, who networks with urban environmentalists around the world, feels that our work can become a national, even international, model, helping to organize conservation coalitions throughout every metropolitan area.

At our next meeting, biologist Ron Klein tells a story about bird-watching when he was a boy. He continues talking, but I am lost in the thought that I have no recollection of ever seeing a bird in my youth. Perhaps I was too busy, the oldest of four, with 26 first cousins, all of whom lived within a few blocks. *Were* there any wild things in Braddock?

The following month I return to Pennsylvania for a wedding, determined to go back to Wood Street, three blocks away from where my mother lives now. I cross the railroad tracks and walk up and down the block. There's one tree, in Peggy Toth's yard, but no birds that I can spot.

Continuing on to visit Aunt Annie and Uncle George, who live next to the steel mill, I suddenly stop. The cooler air of flowing water strikes my face and I realize I am within a few yards of the Monongahela River. I have never been here to see the river, never thought of myself as growing up near a river. It unsettles me to think that I lived the first 20 years of my life in two different houses no more than seven blocks from a river I've never seen. I walk on down to the Monongahela, browned with the look of industrial discharge. Even so, I think about putting in a kayak and exploring someday.

"You walked down to the river!" Aunt Annie admonishes as she pours me a cup of coffee. "Why'd you do that? It's dangerous there."

"Aunt Annie, it's only two blocks away. I can't believe I've never been down there."

"Girls never went there," Uncle George says. "We used to take Denny and Georgie fishing in the '50s. It was really polluted, though.

When your Dad and I were kids, we swam all the time in the Mon. It was real nice back then."

"Don't go down there any more by yourself, Don," Aunt Annie warns, wiping the table. "It's just not safe."

Back on 11th Street, I look up beyond the old St. Michael's Church and the rows of tightly-knit houses to Matta's Hill. Just like the river, it's as though I've never seen it before. A hillside covered with woods, only three streets above Mom's house. I remember that the boys went up there to play, but girls never did. Aunt Annie's cautions stay with me, and I don't trust that it's safe to walk there alone.

At home, I watch my mother tear up stale bread, strewing the pieces on a garbage can lid outside the back door. Before long, sparrows and finches are fighting over the food.

"When did you start feeding birds?" I ask Mom.

"Oh, I've been doing it for years," she answers.

Later, I'm outside staring at the telephone wire when my sister Mary Jane pulls up from work.

"What are you looking at?" she asks.

"That's a mourning dove!"

"Is that what it is? It sits up there all the time."

After a year, I begin to begrudge the part-time FAUNA organizing, hours taken away from interesting scriptwriting projects, from the day-to-day creative storytelling that I've always loved. Then an old client, Odyssey Productions, phones with a full-time project. They've just been awarded a bid to produce two films for the new Oregon Coast Aquarium. One, a story of north Pacific gray whales, will run continuously in its own theater. The other, already titled *Journey of the Raindrop,* will be produced as a 16-monitor videowall for the entranceway. Half a million people are expected to see the shows each year. It's a good time to move on.

There are two very capable women on the Steering Committee who recently left corporate and academic jobs and are looking for conservation work. Julie Weatherby takes a position with Multnomah County Parks, and Mike hires Linda Robinson.

"I never knew what to call myself, " I tell Mike. "Give Linda a title. Call her FAUNA's Director."

When Linda and Mary Rose produce the second directory, there are 287 groups.

I remain on FAUNA's Steering Committee, which has become an official Board of Directors, but I have one commitment that is my own. I'd agreed months ago to conduct a workshop, "Saving Your Own Favorite Space," at the Earth and Spirit Conference.

This is nothing like a revival meeting, but a gentle commingling of a thousand people, Buddhists and Native Americans, theologians and foresters, peace activists and Greens, honoring our spiritual connection to the earth.

We are reminded how far we are removed from harmony with all living things, from ancient traditions that breathe with the balance of nature, from celebrating the abiding sacredness of creation. We look for lessons in New Physics, in indigenous peoples, in Gaia, earth the living organism. Through invoking the spirit of the land, each of us can look to our own deep love of the planet, and whatever ethics guide the myriad parcels of our lives.

It is another gathering of kindred souls, and it is held in a church.

Chapter 10
Birdhouse in the Square

Six weeks before the November election, in September, 1992, the Citizens Campaign for Metropolitan Greenspaces is in deep trouble. A poll just revealed that only 18 percent of the region's voters are even aware of ballot measure 26-1. The referendum would create a small property tax, something like ten cents a day for a $100,000 home, to acquire and protect $200,000,000 of remaining urban natural areas.

The Greenspaces measure has been overshadowed by the heated state referendum Measure 9, which would require discrimination against homosexuals, and the excitement of the Clinton-Bush presidential race. With little money, and even less media exposure, the campaign seems destined for a depressingly overwhelming defeat.

A few friends and I have been disgruntled with the official campaign for quite some time, and whenever we meet, the conversation veers to creative notions of what might be done. Sharing our frustration, Bob comments to me one evening, "There are at least four groups working to fight Measure 9. Why not form our own campaign group?" Not ten minutes later I'm on the phone with Marcia Hoyt, Alison Highberger and Mary Rose: "How about starting our own campaign? We could be The Guerrilla Gang for Greenspaces!" Yes, of course! All the guerrillas decide to meet Saturday for pasta at Ali's.

After two bottles of wine, spicy tomato garlic sauce over herb fettucini and chocolate-laced cookies, we're warmed to the topic.

"We need to create an event that the media can't ignore," Marcia says, drawing from her years of experience as an award-winning advertising manager.

"Yeah," Ali ponders. "It needs to be something really public and dramatic. Like maybe if we tied Mike Houck to the statue in the middle of Pioneer Square for a week."

"It should be something that relates to wildlife, though," Mary Rose adds.

"We could build a giant blue heron's nest at the rookery at Heron Lakes golf course, and he could live in it," Bob suggests.

"Well, it would be better to be located somewhere really public, where a lot of people would see it. And where the television cameras could get there easily. Heron Lakes is too removed," comments Ali, a television producer.

"Why not build a heron nest in Pioneer Square?" Marcia asks, referring to downtown's most popular park, often called the city's Living Room.

"Instead of a heron nest, why not have a giant purple martin house, based on Dave Fouts' design?" I counter.

"That's it!"

Marcia phones Houck to see if he'll do it, but he's in Washington, D.C. She leaves him a message, and we laugh uproariously to imagine him calling from the east coast and hearing this proposition.

"I'll call my neighbor Jeff Joslin to see if he'll be our birdhouse architect," I enthuse.

It's past ten, and after hearing the plans Jeff's first question is, "How many bottles of wine have you been drinking?" He follows that with, "I'm your man!"

Marcia phones the Square first thing Monday, to see if the Birdhouse is even feasible. It is, and the Square's promotion manager seems enamored with the concept. Jeff stops by daily, studying the site and working up preliminary drawings. Construction materials will be donated, but we have to raise about $1,200 to pay for the Square's rental, night security and insurance. Guerrillas that we are, we still don't want to alienate the official campaign or splinter their support, so we meet with their managers, who are so distressed by the poll they welcome contributions of any sort; our energy and good humor become contagious.

Bob suggests we sell campaign buttons at a dollar each and gets a freelance graphic artist to volunteer a design based on the campaign's logo. The artist, himself excited about the project, instead designs eight buttons, and Bob and I front the $430. We press the manufacturer to have half of the 2,500 buttons ready for the Salmon Festival, where nearly 10,000 wildlife watchers come to celebrate the return of the spawning salmon on the Sandy River.

Even before Houck returns, some of his friends are concerned about him living in the middle of downtown Portland in a giant birdhouse. "It doesn't send the right message," one warns, "We don't want to be portrayed as eco-freaks." Another says, "Mike's the key person in this campaign, and it doesn't seem a good use of his time." I trust our judgment, but to be on the safe side, phone Janet Cobb, who mortgaged her house to fund a similar campaign in California in 1988, Measure AA, that raised $225 million for the East Bay Regional Park District in Alameda and Contra Counties, with 38 local city parks also benefiting. She's now the East Bay Parks assistant general manager, and a close friend of Mike's.

"I think it sounds fabulous!" Janet exclaims. "There's no time to waste. When you don't have money, you have to do outrageous things. I'm taking the rest of my vacation days and I'll be up there Monday to help."

We all eventually agree that Mike will stay in the Birdhouse only the first night. We'll hold a press conference with him the following morning, and then other celebrities will live in the Birdhouse the rest of the week, now shortened, for finances' sake, to five days.

Rain plagues the Salmon Festival, and we sell only $392 worth of buttons, not even enough to reimburse their cost. Ali and I, who are the most committed (or daft, however one looks at it), decide that we are each willing to cover up to $600, if need be, to make the Birdhouse a reality. But three days before Jeff's preliminary construction date, we have a major setback. The building firm that we thought was going to donate all the materials misunderstood our request, and only intended to give us some leftover lumber. Jeff estimates that the materials needed will total nearly a thousand dollars. Ali and I agree that we cannot afford to vouch for the extra money.

Janet Cobb's in town and the campaign Steering Committee holds a meeting, which we attend to update everyone. My pride doesn't want to admit that the project may have to fold, but that seems the case. Janet begins the meeting by enthusing profusely about the Birdhouse, and all the publicity it's sure to bring. In dire tones, Ali speaks up about the dollars needed and how the project could die. "If you'd all pitch in, though, we can make it happen!" she encourages. Carol Pinegar—who somehow must have staged this with Ali, although neither will admit it—dramatically tosses a hundred dollars on the table. Mike opens his wallet and adds fifty. Checkbooks emerge—another hundred, 25, 50 dollars, until the pledges total $850, enough to build the Birdhouse. The Guerrilla Gang for Greenspaces is in business.

Marcia and Ali meet for lunch at my place, each with a list of potential Birdhouse-sitting celebrities, the phone in place on the dining room table. One of the first people we call, Jonathan Nicholas, a popular columnist for *The Oregonian*, advises us that it would be a much better news story to have the same person live in the house all five days. It won't matter, he says, whether the person is a celebrity. We shift our tactics. Who might be willing to live in the Birdhouse? I phone two writers—a novelist and playwright—neither is home. On a hunch, Ali calls an acquaintance, Alan Hunter, an enthusiastic outdoorsman with a four-year-old son, who runs a translation business from his home. He thinks it's an exciting idea and almost without hesitation, he agrees.

The Metropolitan Greenspaces Master Plan is a work of wildlife artistry. Two hundred million dollars would be used to buy an emerald necklace of wildlife habitat laced throughout a four-county area. The concept was originally proposed in 1903 by the Olmsteds, renowned landscape architects. Today's Greenspaces Plan is a 1990s high tech version. Photographers were flown over the entire region, shooting infrared squares that pinpointed every remaining greenspace. Then, based on fieldwork by wildlife biologists, computer scientists generated enormous GIS maps of all the region's wetlands, uplands and forests, to a detail of ten acres. Computerized land use data was overlayed to indicate public versus private ownership.

The results are daunting. More than 91 percent of the inventoried natural areas are unprotected, with the potential for becoming condos and shopping malls. The frightening reality is brought home by the reports of the field biologists whose study, conducted only a year after the photography, shows that ten percent of the remaining greenspaces are already developed. Janet Cobb is right: there's no time to waste.

The biologists analyzed the maps and gave recommendations for what should be saved, based on the habitats' biological significance, and their connectedness. Bluffs, buttes, canyons, lakes, ponds, rivers, streams, creeks, marshes, forests, wetlands, lowlands, hills and valleys would be linked together in a green chain of jewels. Regional treasures would be protected, like the forest-cloaked Boring Lava Domes, Cooper Mountain with its rare ponderosa pines, and the Sentinel Tree, a giant Douglas-fir estimated to be at least 300 years old. This is a plan even developers can love, because it means, in essence, that if you save enough connected wildlife habitat, you can develop the rest and still maintain the green quality of life for which Portland and Oregon are renowned.

My fondness for the plan strikes closer to home: I think it will help save Sauvie Island's wildlife habitat. Last year more than 750,000 people visited Sauvie's wildlife areas, a number greater than the visitors to some national parks. Its familiarity, its proximity to downtown Portland draw crowds that seriously impact the viability of the wildlife habitat—mountain bicyclists veering off-road through the thicket of woods, fishermen littering with lines that choke waterfowl, people hacking off tree branches to build fires. Not only that, the rapidly increasing numbers have destroyed the sense of solitude. There are places on the island where, even three years ago, I could walk for an hour without seeing another soul; now dozens of people will pass on those same trails. With the Greenspaces Master Plan in place, there will be a wealth of well-publicized other places for people to go and watch wildlife, places nearer their own neighborhoods, places where they can seek their own solitude.

"Okay, let's move these posts into position," Jeff yells over the clamorous motor of the fork lift. The 500-pound plywood flooring of the Birdhouse is hoisted a few feet in the air, held up by chains suspended from the lift. Jeff shows his diagrams to the crew of seven, who angle the posts accordingly in holes sawn in the floor.

Already past dark, their labors are illuminated by work lights, reflected in the wet bricked pavement of Pioneer Square. City lights, from Nordstrom's, office buildings and the old Courthouse, add a magical touch to the rough-hewn proceedings.

"Watch out!" someone yells as the crew chief deftly operates the lift, raising the floor, which swings slightly, to a height of seven feet. Jeff, wearing a black shirt and jeans, a navy baseball cap, with a tool belt around his waist, swings up on a ladder and drills holes for the massive bolts that connect the floor and posts.

"Be careful of the tools," he admonishes. "They have to be off the ground." Each of Pioneer Square's thousands of bricks is personal, embedded with the name of its donor. Any bricks chipped would have to be replaced, not easily nor inexpensively. So the pieces of the Birdhouse were configured last Saturday at Jeff's island farm, to keep construction work here to a minimum. I imagined everything would be connected in place in an hour or two, but we've been here longer than that already.

Three guys have climbed a ladder up onto the flooring. "I feel like a politician," one of them quips to the crowd of bystanders below. Then one by one, the walls are raised, two sidewalls, next the rear—solid pieces of wood—then the front, with its huge entry hole, giving the structure for the first time the distinct look of a birdhouse. I've seen enough of Jeff's work to recognize his style, sophisticated but a little funky and off-edge. "Right angles are overrated," he says, only half in jest. Yesterday he lost his job; the architecture firm where he worked ran out of projects. He was the last person to be let go. "What timing!" he says with a laugh. "Some people have resumes. I have a giant birdhouse."

"What are you saying's going to be tricky?" the crew chief asks, overhearing part of Jeff's conversation.

"The piece I call 'the tree,'" Jeff explains. "That 16-foot green wedge. It slides through the slot of the roof, but above the roof plane will be the real purple martin birdhouses. They have to get attached there—somehow—after the roof's in place."

Next the fork lift raises the roof. It seems to me to swing precariously, and I'm concerned for the guys inside the walls. The crew chief gently lowers it. "Hold it right there!" someone yells. It stays there, suspended, as the men walk in and out of the hole onto the front deck, looking up. "I think we'll have to cut it," Jeff says. The crew chief gets out from the fork lift and clambers up for a look. Back in the lift, he swings the roof around and down, suspending it about five feet off the ground. Jeff gets beneath it and saws, the roof moving slightly with the force. I watch nervously; if the roof should somehow fall, Jeff would be crushed. Even though the Birdhouse pieces had been built last Saturday, the guys hadn't had time to assemble them, and now the roof doesn't quite fit. When Jeff is satisfied that the problem's been taken care of, the roof is raised again, the guys guiding it upward. The scene has the quality of a barn-raising, the men lifting the pieces into place. A Birdhouse-raising; Ali and I are captivated by its spirit.

It's midnight by the time "the tree" is ready to be moved into place, and only four guys are left. So Ali and I join in, helping to maneuver the 150-pound triangle, everyone yelling directions at once:

"Back it that way— toward us."

"I got too much weight here."

"Don't move!"

"You pull in the bottom."

"Six, eight more inches!"

"Hold it! That's enough!"

Then Jeff rides the tines of the fork life, tied to it, lifted up to the top of "the tree" where he nails a pair of Dave Fouts' purple martin houses in place. It's clear how the human-sized Birdhouse mimics these ten-inch versions.

By two in the morning, the Birdhouse is built. We clean up the tools and everyone who's left walks the stairs at the far end of the Square, looking down at the Birdhouse. "It seems like it belongs there," someone comments. "Like it should stay there forever."

"I can't believe we pulled this off in three weeks," I whisper to Ali.

"If we could do this, Donna, we can do anything!"

"Case for Better Tweetment" headlines Jonathan Nicholas's newspaper story. "No cheep shots, please" is the caption on a photo of Alan and his son in the Birdhouse. Four-year-old Zach stars in television clips, climbing monkey-like in and out of the Birdhouse, while Alan talks about his concern for our disappearing greenspaces. The official campaign staff set up a booth, staffed morning through late evening with volunteers selling buttons, distributing flyers and explaining the measure. In the rush of bringing the Birdhouse into existence, we didn't have time to schedule a full agenda of entertainment, but still managed to arrange for dancers, musicians, Halloween bird-mask making and an appearance by Syd the Red-tailed Hawk.

The evening of the second day I meet Alan for coffee, prepping him for a radio interview tomorrow. During the city's most popular morning drive-time news show, he'll be live on the air from the Birdhouse with Les Sarnoff of KINK radio.

"How's it going?" I ask.

"It's great! People can see me working in there and I come out on the deck and talk. Kids are fascinated. It's been really gratifying. People will come by and say, 'I saw you on TV and wanted to come and support you.'"

"While I was waiting for you I noticed that blond-haired man who walked by and gave you a thumbs-up."

"Little things like that. It's really terrific. A lot of people didn't know about the measure. I've been down where the volunteers are passing out information. The response is overwhelmingly positive."

"What's it like inside the Birdhouse? Cramped?"

"No, it's comfortable. There's room for the drafting table and futon. Some friends have even come up to visit. One thing, though, that was totally unexpected. Because of the vent holes they drilled in the ceiling, the light comes in from all directions. When I go to sleep, it looks like stars or lightning bugs. A total surprise."

"What does Zach think of it?"

"Zach loves being in the house. Someone asked him what kind of bird he is and he said he's an eagle. I think he'll be really sad when he has to leave. He was listening to me talking about how we need to save greenspaces for the next generations, so now he pokes his head out and tells people, "Vote Yes for me!"

Election night, I wait until past nine to go down to the campaign headquarters. Clinton has already accepted the presidency, but none of the local TV stations even bothered to give figures for Ballot Measure 26-1. We're ahead when I arrive, just barely, and the tone is jubilant. I recognize dozens of people who've worked on the plan since the Greenspaces program began. As the district results dribble in, the winning edge decreases, and finally disappears. When I leave around midnight, it doesn't look encouraging. The next day I can't find the results in the newspaper, so I phone campaign headquarters. YES: 230,100. NO: 287, 778.

YES: 44.4 percent. Not bad, considering. In other places, similar measures were put on the ballot two or three times before they passed. We'll have a strong chance next time, since election results will show us how people voted, district by district, and we only need to change the minds of 2.9 percent of the voters, many of whom were likely uninformed, or ill-informed about the measure. Six days after the election, *The Oregonian* publishes an editorial, "Try Again on Greenspaces." It concludes, "We can't save what is already gone. The region must act soon to save its natural treasures before they disappear forever."

Out-of-pocket expenses for the Birdhouse in the Square come to nearly $2,700. Adding the pledges and button sales, we're still $750 short. Ali and I write a letter to 75 possible contributors, saying "We went out on a limb" and ask them to each send us ten dollars. Almost to the penny, our balance is cleared. Jeff has found a new job, with the architecture firm that designed Pioneer Square.

Metropolitan Greenspaces will be placed on the ballot again. I'm hoping the measure will be called 26-1, so we can sell the remaining 1,400 buttons sitting in a box in my office. At a dinner at our house a few weeks ago, with homemade ravioli and two bottles of wine, the Guerrilla Gang toyed with the notion of a Wildlife Walk—hundreds, no, thousands, of people in animal costumes parading through all the communities.

Just another cheep shot for greenspaces.

Chapter 11
In Wild Waters

"I think you'd better call the sheriff," my mother-in-law Edith said softly.

She, Bob and I had just returned from the last of Christmas shopping; it was 10:15 Saturday night, December 21st. She'd stood in the doorway of my office, intently listening as I played back the messages on my phone machine.

Number one: "Yeah. Donna, it's time for you to leave Sauvies Island, you ugly bitch. I mean, you've done more than your fair share so leave. Otherwise you're gonna have very serious problems goodbye."

Number two: "Hah! Thwaaaaaaaaaaaaa. Rrrr."

Number three: very garbled, like the person had a kerchief wrapped around his mouth: "Thanks a lot from Burlington, Oregon. We really like your goddam *(undecipherable)* especially the *(undecipherable)* open up to the public one certain *(undecipherable)* goddam garbage in the roadway. Dank you Donna. We really appreciate you, moving up here where you came from out of the gutter."

Number four: "Yes, George Seagull. I'd like a book order, uh, pork, uh, dalmation up the ass. So if you'd please send me a copy of it, I'd really like it thank you."

Number five: YahYahYahYahYahWhyYaWhyYa...

Number six: Heavy breathing, then "Huuuuuuuuuuuuuuuuu..."

Number seven: "You made some people very mad down here. I

hope you don't have a good holiday. In fact, a lot of people think you ought to have a really bad holiday. Nobody likes you out here. You came out here. You stuck your nose in everybody's business like you owned the goddamned place. Nobody knows where you came from, so why don't ya just *leave*. Instead'a keep pushin', okay. So either get along with everybody or get outta everybody's business. Bitch!"

Number eight: "You ugly bitch. Talk for yourself. Because nobody else wants to be insulted."

"Call the sheriff," Edith repeated. To please her, I dialed the non-emergency number, certain I'd be told these inane rantings were no big deal. The Sheriff Department's dispatcher asked whether I'd been threatened.

"Well, he said things like 'You better leave town or you're going to have serious problems.' Would you like me to rewind the tape and play it so you can hear?"

"No. I'll send a sheriff out. It's a big party night so he might not get there right away. How late will you be awake?"

"We'll stay up until he comes."

In a surprisingly short time, maybe 45 minutes, two deputies arrived and listened to the tape. They both agreed there were two men talking, not one, and that they were quite drunk. My phone message had said I would be out of the office for the holidays until January 1st and I asked the deputies if I should change it.

"Definitely."

Did I have any idea who it was? Yes, I did. At the Fish and Wildlife CRMP meeting earlier in the week, a man had been especially obnoxious to me. From the time I'd met him, he made it clear he considered me an enemy. Did I recognize his voice on the tape? No.

"There's really nothing we can do at this point," one of the deputies said. "Unless there's a direct threat, the sheriff's office won't monitor your phone calls. If this keeps up, you can pay to have the phone company run a trace. But it's expensive."

They left, and Bob uncorked a bottle of cabernet. The three of us sat up a while longer, at first a bit unsettled, but soon laughing at Kitty Buttons, tangled in Christmas ribbons.

Three weeks later I'm rethinking that incident in one of my best thinking places, the kayak. It's January 20, 1992, the day after hunting season, when the wildlife area first opens again to the public and Howard's leading our traditional Martin Luther King Day paddle. An old friend, Mike Moen, and I are the only two who showed up.

One year it was below freezing and our paddles cracked the ice into thin glassy shards, the surface next to our boats etched in thousands of feathery fractures. Today the weather's mild, near 45 degrees, but windy and overcast.

We're floating on the Gilbert, a narrow meandering river, its headwaters in the center of the island in Sturgeon Lake, emptying about six miles later into the Multnomah Channel. Along the way, it flows past Big Martin Lake, Seal Lake, Pete's Slough, Aaron Lake, Crane Lake, and Big and Little McNary Lakes. On a map, the water patterns look like splashes of dribbling color swung from a painter's hasty brush.

Rounding a bend, we watch a crow harass a bald eagle perched on a high limb, flying directly at him. The eagle flaps its wings in annoyance. The crow charges again. And again. Finally the eagle takes off, and the smaller black bird settles in its place. A minute later, the eagle returns and aggressively bombards the crow, who immediately flees. We look back after a few strokes to see the scene repeat itself.

What of harassment? What of intimidation? What of fear? What of danger? The old questions return, in overlapping layers. Edith's concerns trouble me. I know people whose lives and livelihoods have been threatened by their activism; we all know of people who have been killed. Perhaps I take these threats too lightly. Is it selfish to continue on with nonchalance, without considering the effects on my family? They support me, I know, but still they're alarmed. It's difficult for them to resist wanting me to pull back—just like the man said—"get outta everybody's business." But it's just *because* it's everybody's business that I'm in it. These 12,000 acres of wildlife habitat should be protected for the generations to come. For everybody, not just the few who are furious that their special treatment, which has been to the detriment of wildlife, might come to an end. Harassment is like blackmail. Do what we tell you, or else. Or else what? Wherever my personal line of fear might be drawn, I recognize it's not at two drunks on a Saturday night, hiding behind the anonymity of a telephone. Cowardly creeps, I think, and paddle on.

Wakes from speeding boats have caused the Gilbert's shoreline to be horribly eroded, high banks denuded, tangled tree roots suspending their gnarled fists above the waterway, branches protruding mid-river.

The boughs are fine resting spots for great blue herons, though. When we see them in the distance we stop paddling and float. Great blues are the most skittish of all waterbirds. In one wetlands study by the Romberg Tiburon Center of San Francisco State University, they took flight when a person was 195 feet away. Belding's savannah sparrows flew off at 80 feet, killdeer and coots, 15 to 40 feet. Sometimes the herons will skip on from one spot to the next, branch-hopping ahead of us downriver. Other times they'll buzz low overhead, with their incessant screeching *skwr-a-a-a-rk, skwr-a-a-a-rk*. We've counted as many as 32 great blue herons on a day's paddle along the length of the Gilbert. At night, they roost near Frenchman's Bar, at a protected rookery east and a little north of here on the Columbia.

That wasn't the first time I'd been harassed. One of my favorites was an old woman's phone call.

The Sunday before Halloween, a huge traffic jam caused by pumpkin hunters at island farms bottled up island traffic for hours. The following morning the island made news on another front: an article in *The Oregonian* warned "Critics say livestock policies major threat for Sauvie Island." Biologists were quoted, describing how cattle grazing on ODFW's wildlife area trampled bird nests, polluted lakes and destroyed riparian habitat along shorelines. Although I'd given the reporter, Kathie Durbin, a file of background information, I asked her not to quote me and I stayed out of photographer Michael Lloyd's shots. I wanted to keep myself removed from the story, not for fear of being harassed, but in the hope of avoiding antagonism that would hinder my ability to negotiate with ODFW for improved wildlife habitat.

Even so, I came back from a meeting to an anonymous phone message, an old woman's cracking voice: "Mrs. Matrazzo (sic), I see you're screening your calls again. I hope you're happy with the mess that you're creating. I don't know where it's all going to lead to. Yesterday's display of traffic certainly doesn't compare to what a poor insignificant golf course would give us, 1,200 feet on a country road. I directed some of your birdwatchers off the island. They asked me what was the fastest way off. I told them there was no fastest way. I'd like to direct *you* off the island, but I don't imagine that's possible. Well, have a good day."

I played the tape at our next Conservancy gathering. Everyone howled with laughter as they recognized the woman's voice, because she'd spoken at numerous public hearings. Melissa Marsland shook her head and said, "You know, it's almost sweet."

I'm paddling with a meditative rhythm, chuckling about that call. Wouldn't it be devilish, I muse, to conspire with the filmmakers who are creating an island documentary. They had interviewed this woman; what if they showed her interview, then followed it with me playing this audio tape, her voice a perfect match, her character laid bare.

Although we're about 70 miles from the ocean, the Gilbert moves with the tides. On a day's paddle the length of the river, all the way up and back, a tide table is a necessity. We try to leave when the tide's coming in, four hours before slack, and ride the moon's pull in both directions.

The Gilbert's one of the natural drainage courses on the island, along with Cunningham Slough and Dairy Creek. Before the building of the dikes, when the island used to flood once or twice a year, the river was a siphon that flushed water from the lowlands and small lakes. The 1941 "Big Dike" cut off the southern end of the Gilbert, and three lakes—Little Sturgeon, Marquam and Mouse—began to dry up. They're gone now.

I'm edgy as we near the river's headwaters to verge back onto Sturgeon Lake. The Gilbert's been a refuge today, flat water amidst a sea of whitecaps on the big lake. When we made the open crossing to get here, I had to paddle furiously to keep my boat perpendicular to the waves, certain that the force of a pummeling from the side would swamp me. Howard and Mike, stronger, more experienced paddlers, had no problem. In fact, they relish the challenge, which is why we're heading back a longer, less protected route.

Three miles separate us from the takeout, a half mile of that the open crossing. We surge into the lake, wind whooshing, waves doubling over themselves, lapping into frothy whitecaps. The water is wild, wilder than anything I've ever been in with a sea kayak. As I maneuver through the waves, the roiling waters sweep up from behind, lifting the back of the boat, propelling me forward in a rush, like a surfboard speeding down the face of a crashing, crushing wave. Before I can relax, another's back there, lifting, jouncing, shoving me out of control. I watch as the duck decoy Mike found and gave me, which I'd attached to the bow by bungy cords, is loosened by the breaking waves, then sucked into the watery stew.

Howard and Mike are far enough ahead that they wouldn't be much help should I make a "wet exit"—a misleadingly benign phrase for a dump into frigid water, anything not attached, gone. A boat without proper flotation is sunk as well.

Mike paddles into a grove of flooded trees, and thinking that he's gone there for security, I follow. There, the force of the waves thrashes my boat against the trees. The rudder feels meaningless. I struggle with my strokes, using whitewater sweeps and draws to keep me from slamming against the living buoys. Carefully I wend my way closer to Mike, and find out that he had a cramp in his arm and casually stopped to give it a rest.

Late one evening, Bob fumes into the living room, tossing the cordless telephone onto the sofa.

"Who was that?" I ask with puzzlement.

"Some guy at Delta Park."

"Who?"

"Some guy. Actually, he sounded real…he sounded like a normal person. Here's how the conversation went:

'Hello? How are you? I got your name at Delta Park.'

'Huh?'

'And I'm interested.'

'What?'

'Is your wife's name Donna?'

'Yeah.'

'You're not interested in a threesome?'

'No, not hardly.'

'Sorry to bother you. Goodbye.'"

"Geez. What do you think that was all about?"

"Donna, obviously somebody wrote our name and phone number in the men's room at Delta Park."

I don't know how to answer. The phone rings again. Bob picks it up.

Another man: "I got your name off the wall."

Bob seethes, "What?!"

"Sorry, wrong number."

Bob slams the phone. "If it weren't so late I'd got out and scrub whatever that is off right now." He shake his head. "But I guess it can wait until morning. I'll take some cleaning stuff to work with me."

"What do you think?" I ask.

"I don't know." He walks over to where I'm sitting and wraps his arms around me. "But don't worry about it."

When he stops at Delta Park the next morning, nothing is there.

Easing my way out of the trees, I head back into the main part of the lake, trying to find balance. By the time I've reached the center of the open crossing, I can sense the rhythm of the waves, their regular pulsing, and my place in them. The kayak begins to feel like an extension of me, a body suit; seated low in the water, I'm part of it, moving with it. My strokes feel stronger, more controlled, pulling me with some measure of grace through the sequence of whitecaps.

When I land, I realize I'd been so engrossed in reaching shore I forgot I'd only be as far as the Narrows, with the West Arm of Sturgeon and Steelman yet to cross. Mike and Howard, wind-combed and energized, wait to help me portage my kayak across the dike. The three of us paddle the rest of the way together, the smaller, more sheltered lakes almost serene.

On an August Wednesday, returning to my office, I find an anxious plea from a wildlife biologist to please call her back today, and she adds her home phone.

She had come at my request to testify on behalf of the Conservancy at a public hearing to protect an important wetland. I'd called her afterwards to thank her, telling her that she was a strong, charismatic speaker and her testimony was powerful.

"I was really nervous," she confided.

Today she has something else to be nervous about. The developers filed a formal complaint against her to her employer, a government agency, accusing her of misrepresenting her position.

"Look, I clearly remember you started your testimony by saying you were speaking as a private citizen. And the county has an audio tape we can get and transcribe."

"Would you write a letter for me that I can use in my response to the complaint?"

"I'll send it today," I answer, and add, "That's a really vengeful and rotten thing for them to do. Could it hurt your job?"

"Well, sure. I could lose my job. And it's not easy for a biologist to find a job these days."

"That makes me angry. It makes me really angry that we work so hard and then people threaten us. They try to intimidate us. It's only because you were so good that they did that."

"Don't worry about me. Even if I lose my job. That's why I chose this career, because wildlife can't speak out for itself. I see that as my role in life. I'm not sorry for speaking up."

"Yeah, I know what you mean. I'm never sorry, either."

Nights of no stars, days of shrouded sun.
Pittsburgh steel mill, c. 1950. Courtesy Carnegie Library of Pittsburgh.

Instilling do-goodness.
Author with parents, Tarz
and Gert Matrazzo, in
Wood Street house on
Confirmation day.

A day to fall in love with an island. Paddling on Sturgeon Lake, Mount St. Helens in the background.

Trillium Woods. Not in Braddock anymore.

Godfather of Greenspaces.
Mike Houck at Oaks Bottom wetlands, one of the many natural areas in the region he helped to protect.

Dinner for eight, view from desk.
Hummingbird feeder just outside the office window.

Matching life jackets. The author and pal Jibo.

An eye for all the best outdoors spots. Bob Stephens and Mount Hood.

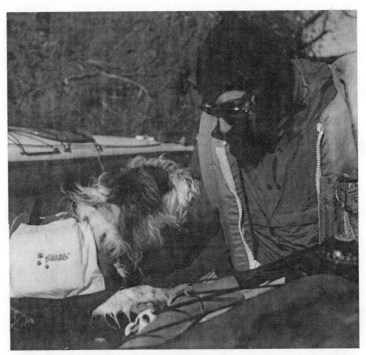

Two salty sea dogs. Howard Blumenthal, favorite treat-giver of all Jibo's paddling pals.

The Purple Martin Man. Dave Fouts checking purple martin gourds at Howell Territorial Park.

Jim Charlton and Sage. Beside the lake at Charlton Farms.

"A Citizen Who Cares." Television public service announcement that aired statewide.

Birdhouse in the Square. Desperately seeking publicity for the first greenspaces bond measure.

Young in the act. Lily Joslin, age 4-1/2, helping paint the Birdhouse.

The Guerrilla Gang for Greenspaces. Jeff Joslin, Mike Houck, Janet Cobb, Rich Carson, Alison Highberger, the author, Mary Rose Navarro, Brian Cosgrove.

Media spokesperson. Finding the courage to speak up for the land in a very public way.

Guerrilla Girls Over Time and Place. Ali Highberger and the author visiting Marcia Hoyt and Lantz House.

Ready to campaign. Malina McKenzie wearing a Citizens for Metropolitan Greenspaces T-shirt.

Skydrea McKenzie. At the writer's cabin, back from a hike at Walden Farm.

Jesse McKenzie. Baking Christmas cookies.

Earth Sisters. Mary Rose Navarro, Lily Joslin and the bridesmaid author at Leach Botanical Gardens.

House for Autumn. Artist Helen Lessick's temporary hay bale structure. © Helen Lessick

PART 3
CHANGE

Chapter 12
Still Teed Off

"No wonder the Japanese want to build a golf course here," Jerome says, waving a magazine article like a flag. "Listen to this," he reads: "Want to play golf in Japan? Got a million?...Prices for memberships peaked at about $3.5 million at one of Tokyo's most exclusive clubs, and at $80,000 to a million at others." He looks up. "It's cheaper for the Japanese to fly back and forth to play golf on Sauvie than to play in Japan."

"They're saying it won't be a private Japanese golf club," I counter.

"There's nothing to stop them," Jack insists.

Dave walks in, still caked with dirt from working the fields. "I was hoping I wouldn't be too late." He tosses a check for $500 on the table. "L.C. Jacobson—we lease a lot of our Sauvie land from him—donated this. He's going to send his manager up for the hearing. I'd like to save five minutes of our 45 minutes of testimony for him."

"Well this solves one big problem," Stu says with elation, eyeing the check. "Now we can hire our own traffic consultant."

Betsy warns, "We're already squeezing half a dozen people into our testimony time."

"Don't worry, Dave advises. "Wait until you meet Elden."

As I increasingly become the spokesperson for the Conservancy, quoted in newspapers and on television, a long-time resident becomes my counterpart, speaking out in support of the golf course. I soon recognize that my quotes can't match hers in entertainment value.

Under a headline of "Islanders want golfers," her letter was published in *The Oregonian*:

> To the Editor: Sauvie Island is going to have a golf course. The residents want this course. There is only a small, very vocal, non-island group that is against it. It has been cleverly orchestrating and manipulating the media into believing we residents are against it. We have been the silent majority long enough. I want all 200 acres of the golf course.
>
> The birds already have 11,371 acres of Sauvie Island outright. They use the rest as they please and will continue to do so. The ducks and geese are not only beautiful, but have more sense than their self-proclaimed protectors.

In a newspaper interview, she is quoted as saying the new golf course will bring "desirable people" to the island, and adds, "I think the character of the island could certainly use some cleaning up."

My favorite is a television interview in which she declares, "In my opinion, they're professional rabble-rousers, because they are against anything. Not that they have anything to do with it. They haven't lived here and paid taxes."

I laughed to a friend, "I haven't been called so many names since third grade."

Five days before the hearing, a 700-word essay I submitted to *The Oregonian*, "Limit Size of Sauvie Golf Course" is featured on the editorial pages. It concludes with this statement:

> If we must have a golf course, let it be restricted to the original 125 acres. A course of that size is not

likely to have major tournament potential. We might
contain the domino effect of commercial development
that would surely follow a tournament course—
development that would eventually spell doom for the
wildlife that Oregonians want very much to protect.

"A former state supreme court justice called me yesterday," Betsy
begins, at our rehearsal the evening before the hearing. "He's very fond
of Sauvie Island, and he's offered to come and speak on our behalf. I
know we're pressed for time, but I couldn't turn him down."

"We can cut out my testimony," I offer. Jerome and Carolyn agree
to splice their time as well.

"We don't want to eliminate anything," Betsy says. "We'll just have
to edit more—and talk fast."

"How precise does it have to be?" I ask.

"They run a stopwatch," Jerome says, "and when the time's up, a
buzzer sounds and all you're allowed to do is finish the sentence you've
started."

"By the way," Betsy adds, "I finally got a chance to check on the
cases they cited. None of them showed any liability regarding safety
and golf course sites.

"So here's the lineup: I'll talk about why the safety issue is a legal
farce. Let's put the former justice on next. Followed by Stu and the
traffic consultant's report. Then Dave, and the lack of 'substantial
construction.' Donna and tournament statistics. Carolyn and wildlife
data. Jerome and chemicals. After listening to Elden's notes, I think we
should save him for last. Then I'll finish with a summary."

Jack says, "That gives everybody about five minutes each. I brought
a stopwatch; let's try a run-through."

About 75 people gather in the county commissioners' Board Room
the day of the hearing. The front seat is filled with folks wearing "Golf
Course/YES" buttons, the rear section full of people in opposition. As
with the earlier hearing, television cameras and reporters line the far
wall.

The developers squander much of their 45 minutes with a consultant showing traffic diagrams. Our fast-moving, passionate, well-researched presentations provide a lively counterpoint. I end my testimony with a flamboyant naming of each of the 17 lanes that exit the Coliseum. "And how many lanes are there leaving Sauvie? (dramatic pause) One." The crowd bursts into applause, which is immediately chastised by the commission chairwoman, banging her gavel to regain order. Returning to my seat, I stifle a grin.

Elden von Lehe's presentation is last. In his crisply ironed dress shirt, jeans and boots, he takes the podium and booms, "Who will speak for the land?" He describes his firm's commitment to farming, and how they restored two large barns on Sauvie at great expense. "Who will speak for the land?" He points out Sauvie's value as the most productive farmland of all their operations. "Who will speak for the land?" he repeats, explaining how urban development encourages speculators and discourages farmers. He predicts that the increased taxes, higher land valuation and impacts on surrounding farms would eventually drive agriculture from Sauvie Island. He ends by saying that the question here is not just about a golf course, but will the county break faith with the noble goal of preserving the island's unique land for food production.

At the beginning of the hearing, the county commissioners announced they would not make a decision that day, because the issues were so complex. Our testimony, however, makes it clear that the applicant has not met his "burden of proof." Then commissioner Rick Bauman presses the farmer's attorney into undermining their own position. If, as they say, their sole reason for wanting the expansion to 200 acres is safety, will they still build the golf course whether or not the expansion is approved? The answer is yes.

That clinches it. The county commissioners decide to vote, and our appeal carries, three to one.

The decision comes so fast we're caught off guard; before I know it I'm stammering into a television camera. We're all so exhilarated we can't detach ourselves to go our separate ways, so we head to a restaurant where we can barely stop talking to eat. It seems not too far-fetched to hope that the developers, now thwarted from building a multimillion dollar golf course, won't invest that kind of money in a small, rural-style one, and maybe it won't be worthwhile to build one at all. Later, watching the evening news, I'm still so euphoric that I can laugh at my own wide-eyed babbling.

Two days after our victory, the farmer's attorney files a formal complaint against Betsy to the Oregon State Bar, stating that she "unfairly accused my client of unethical conduct and implied fraudulent and even possibly criminal conduct, causing irreparable harm to my client."

I read his accusations and think it's a joke, but Betsy, the daughter of an attorney who has fought the golf course *pro bono*, isn't amused. We have no doubt she'll be cleared of the allegations, but the complaint itself remains in her file forever.

The attorney writes, for example, that "Ms. Newcomb stated that there was the appearance of impropriety, thus a new hearing should be ordered." In fact, Betsy didn't ask for a new hearing, she simply requested some latitude in determining what was on the record.

He says "the issue of unethical behavior had been raised as of March 12th by Ms. Newcomb's clients [Stu and Jerome] with the planning director." That date was a Sunday, and both Jerome and Stu deny any such conversation.

Based on this supposed conversation, the attorney accuses Betsy of knowing about the issue for two months in advance of the hearing and that she "had an affirmative duty to promptly notify the Board of the alleged conduct. Instead, she chose the most prejudicial time to my client's reputation to make her false accusation." In reality, we hadn't received a copy of the transcripts from the county until a week before the hearing, and Betsy never saw them until the night before the hearing.

At Betsy's request, I write a letter to the Oregon Bar. My letter advises the Disciplinary Council to listen to the tape of the hearing, so they'll realize the entire intent of these accusations is misguided. The County Commissioners did not order a new hearing because there was the appearance of impropriety. They requested it solely because they felt the tapes were inaudible.

The complaint is investigated, and Betsy is cleared.

Three weeks before our appeals hearing, the county commissioners meet to issue the Final Order reversing the decision of the Planning Commission. Their Findings of Fact are based on the essence of our testimony: That the proposed expansion is inconsistent with the character of the area. The applicant didn't prove that a 200-acre golf course would not have an adverse affect on natural resources. That such a golf course *would* have an adverse affect on surrounding agricultural lands, and aggravate the existing traffic problems on the island.

The Findings conclude, "Many golf courses operate safely on substantially less acreage. The expansion of the golf course beyond what is needed for the proposed use is inconsistent with the land use objectives for this district, i.e., preservation of agricultural lands in large blocks and minimizing non-agricultural uses."

As the commissioners accept the Findings and sign the Final Order, we wait anxiously to hear how they will respond to a six-page request from Betsy's law firm, hand-delivered five days ago, to determine whether the 1983 Conditional Use permit has expired.

The commissioners turn to their county counsel, Larry Kressel, who has researched the matter and issues an opinion. His research, he reports, doesn't disclose a definitive answer, but he feels it would be risky for the county to revisit the issue at this late date. He is concerned that if the Board reversed the director's 1983 position and then the farmer sued the county, the court's sympathy would lay with the farmer. He also points out that doubt could be cast on other rulings by the planning director. The county commissioners agree to follow his advice, and allow the 1983 permit to remain valid.

One month after our hearing, the farmer appeals the county's decision to LUBA, the state Land Use Board of Appeals. On behalf of Jerome, Bob, Carolyn, Stu, Jack and me, Betsy files a motion to intervene, stating "as persons who appeared before the Planning Commission and the Board of County Commissioners, the prospective intervenors have a substantial stake in the outcome of this appeal."

It becomes ironic, that we who began by fighting Multnomah County, now become allies in helping the county defeat the appeal. Betsy writes a brief on our behalf.

To do so, she reads through more than 1,200 pages of material, more than once, to organize her points. Her 26-page brief begins by stating that we "challenge all remarks" made by the petitioners. Some of her comments are followed by as many as 33 references to the record. In essence, the farmer's attorney continually argues that the *county* didn't provide enough evidence. Betsy counters that "this approach is fundamentally wrong; it is the applicant's burden to show that the criteria have been satisfied as a matter of law." She contends that their attorney's arguments demonstrate a fundamental misunderstanding of the standards for challenging a denial, and this flaw pervades all of their arguments. She and Kressel feel confident the county's denial will be upheld.

The LUBA hearing is held in the state capital, Salem, an hour's drive south of Portland. Betsy pointed out to the Conservancy that LUBA referees are definitely not swayed by support or opposition in the audience, so no one else but me decides to make the trip.

Despite the farmer, his wife and friends seated in the row behind me, I feel confident. The farmer's attorney speaks first, and notes that he has years of experience with land use cases, and this is Betsy's first. Larry Kressel speaks next, in a low-key voice, for just a few minutes. He stresses what it is that the LUBA attorneys seek, and states that the farmer's attorneys misunderstood the role of LUBA.

Betsy begins by saying the attorney is correct—this is her first land use case. "Trial by fire," she comments. But, she continues, "that might be a good thing, because I don't have anything to compare it to. All I can do is what I'm trained to do—look at the standards." Point by point, she counters the lawyers' contentions and I can't help but notice that the LUBA attorneys seem to be listening intently, taking more notes from her comments than anyone else's.

As people shuffle in leaving, I hear a voice just behind me complain about newcomers who don't know what's going on and try to change everything. Then as the owner of this voice, a gray-haired woman, passes me, she whips around and shoves her cane in my face saying, "That includes you."

Leaning over me, she tells me that I don't know anything. I retort that I suspect she doesn't know very much about what would happen if that golf course came in.

"We need that golf course."

"Farmers don't need golf courses."

"Yes we do."

"Then why," I ask, "are farmers around the world fighting against golf courses on farmlands?"

"They're not," she says. "And what about all those nude bathers?" She's referring to the people who come to the clothing-optional beach along the Columbia River.

"What about them? What harm do you think they're doing?"

She whispers, "They crap on people's lawns."

"Naked people crapping on lawns! Do you have any pictures?" She harrumphs and walks away.

I walk downstairs with Betsy and Kressel. "I think we've got it made on this one," he says quietly.

Indeed we have. We win on all eight issues of the appeal, and LUBA's Final Order and Opinion is replete with statements that begin, "We agree with respondents…"

If we had any thought of disbanding the Sauvie Island Conservancy after the Final Order, they were soon waylaid by a request to investigate the dumping of radioactive zirconium sand on the island. Then we were offered a position on the county's Bicycle Task Force. Mike Houck called about ODFW's plan to institute a parking permit fee, which for the first time would allow wildlife-watchers to pay for part of the wildlife area expenses. As supporters, we were asked to testify in favor of the plan before the state's Fish and Wildlife Commission. From there the work has never stopped. In fact, it has hardly ever slowed.

Jeanne's presence at the hearing triggered a fallout with her aunt and cousin, and she sadly found herself no longer invited to family meals. For her, the island polarization struck home.

The golf course was never built. First the parent company in Japan declared bankruptcy. Eventually, unable to find a buyer by the deadline in their agreement with the farmer, the firm deeded the land back to him, losing about $600,000 in the process. We were delighted to read that all prospective buyers backed away from the project because they feared too much opposition. Now it cannot be built, because two years have passed since a new state law prohibiting golf courses on prime farmland went into effect. According to the new statute, the lack of development invalidates the Conditional Use permit.

Proposals for the island have appeared non-stop, including a multimillion dollar marina, and a 1,600-bed women's prison. Our hard-earned lessons have helped us to battle with savvy and strength.

Our group has grown well, I think. Our meetings have morphed into a monthly Dinner Collective, politics served with meals around someone's dinner table, heaped with caring and energy between mouthfuls of shiitake risotto and chocolate-covered rum cakes. We have no elected officers, but a loosely organized Board, every person considered a leader. We operate in two modes, Crisis, or Isn't it Time to Get Together? We make no demands of one another. Each contributes what he or she is willing to do. I think that through each other, we have all found courage. But I can only speak for myself: I've learned to replace anger with action, frustration with research, quiet complaints with a bold and public face.

My knees don't shimmy at public hearings anymore.

Chapter 13
The Rescue of Steelman Lake: Field Notes

M ARCH FIFTEENTH, 1992

"Get down to Steelman as soon as you can. You won't believe what happened."

"What?" I ask with anxiety.

"I can't describe it. You just have to see it."

That's all Howard was inclined to say last night, so I wait with unease until Bob gets home from work, unwilling to face Steelman alone. Late afternoon we drive to the lake, one of my favorite spots on the island, or anywhere, for that matter. The shoreline is almost unrecognizable. Its small turnaround and stile have been replaced with a massive parking lot surrounded by—I'm obsessed with counting them—117 boulders. Bulldozed into the lake is a full-sized boat ramp. A seven-foot-wide trail has been cleared and graded through the mid-riparian zone, just beneath the trees where we know bald eagles perch to forage.

I have trouble sleeping, then fitfully dream: Bob and I are living on the north end of the island, where I notice something being built, an all-white two-story building with a patio of colonnades, like some

Roman theater. "I have to go and see what it is," I tell Bob. Beyond the patio I come to a large modern glass-windowed office building. On the bottom floor is a restaurant, with employees carrying trays of the disposables I despise—paper plates and cups, paper napkins, plastic forks. The place is still under construction but filled with people, and already amok with litter. I walk upstairs, the expanse piled with chairs and room dividers, soon to be office cubicles. I decide to bomb the place.

When I wake up I'm taut with fury.

It's not as though I didn't know something was coming. A few months ago I was on a Bald Eagle Watch standing at Coon Point listening to Mike Golden, the deputy director of Oregon's Department of Fish and Wildlife, describe plans to improve the wildlife viewing opportunities at the Point and Steelman Lake. Nothing seemed imminent and I assumed our CRMP group would be involved in any development. Just the same, I kept trying to contact the agency's busy public affairs director, whom Mike said could give me more information. Yesterday's mail brought a copy of the plan. I was stunned. It showed a $93,663 development with a 1-1/2 mile trail, three cement viewing blinds and an interpretive kiosk. The project, entitled "Steelman Viewing Trail," and illustrated by a couple of scribbly grade-school-style sketches, was scheduled to begin construction in "fiscal year 93."

MARCH TWENTY-FOURTH

The "Save Steelman!" campaign begins. Even though the Conservancy had so much success with the media during the golf course battle, we decide to first try and work with ODFW to halt further development and dismantle what's been done. We've learned, though, that construction contracts have already been signed. So we send a letter to agency director Randy Fisher, with copies to other ODFW managers and non-game staff, and to environmental, wildlife, boating and other organizations. A notice at the bottom advises that if no action is taken immediately, we will contact the media.

Among other things, the letter says, "By building a boat ramp, accompanied by such a huge parking lot, you've guaranteed that Steelman will be clogged shore to shore with every kind of recreational water vehicle—powerboats, jet skis, motorized rafts—you name it. Already fishermen trolling in motorboats have been seen out there. No question, the wildlife will all be gone."

Oregon has more than 6,000 lakes. But very few are "quiet waters," lakes without motorized boats. The guidebook *Oregon's Quiet Waters* lists only one major lake within 30 miles of the city of Portland. A small quiet lake like Steelman is only about 20 miles from downtown, which is why it's so treasured. In the past, if you wanted to paddle at Steelman, you had to make numerous trips with your gear raised over your head as you walked through a narrow stile. Then two people, one on either side, would slide the kayak over a four-foot cattle fence, wending your way through cowpies as you lugged everything to the water's edge. In winter you crackled through a rim of ice, in summer the mud sucked and swallowed your sandals if you weren't careful. But once you're afloat, Steelman has been a place to quietly savor silence punctuated by birdsong. Its calmness made it a place for meditation, a place for learning how to handle a boat, a place for pouring out your heart, and because of it a place I've often taken other women.

I feel confident as a boatswoman now, but it wasn't always so. I can remember my earliest days of paddling with the Pittsburgh hostel group. With no athleticism, weak arm muscles, no water skills, I felt awkward and inept. I could barely lift the canoe onto car-top boat racks. And then there was that knot. To tie a boat securely, first you attach a rope somewhere on the right underside of the car, pass it through a hook at the boat's bow, then just above the car's hood, take a stretch of rope, fold it and tie a sort-of noose. The end of the rope is looped somewhere on the left underside of the car, making a triangle. But to hold the rope taut and the boat steady, you need to draw up that loose end, bring it through the noose and tie a particular kind of half hitch knot. I never could remember it. Every time I went on a paddling trip, with embarrassment I'd have to ask someone to show me again. Then one day, I had a canoe all ready—and I stopped. Without realizing it, I had remembered and tied the knot correctly. I'd already learned how to maneuver a canoe, paddle the J-stroke, use sweep and draw strokes through rapids, but it was the day I naturally knew how to tie the knot that I felt I'd truly become a boatwoman. Steelman had been a place for nurturing that in others.

The "extinction of experience," that's what writer Robert Michael Pyle calls it. Just as surely as the demise of the passenger pigeon, the experience of Steelman became extinct.

MARCH TWENTY-FIFTH

At our CRMP meeting, I agree with Jim Charlton's request that ODFW stop all development until the current planning process is complete, and ask that the boat ramp be removed. Others concur.

APRIL FIRST

Without any encouragement from ODFW, I contact Kathie Durbin, the environmental reporter for *The Oregonian*. She said she'd heard about the controversy and asked if I could show her around.

APRIL SIXTH

My amateur-naturalist's instinct tells me that such development is harmful to wildlife. How can I prove it? So I embark on a research study, not unlike what I do in my work of writing educational films. I interview a wildlife biologist, planner, naturalist, landscape designer and wildlife habitat designer, among others.

From them I learn, for example, that the trail is in the worst possible place. Putting a trail halfway up the bank breaks the habitat chain. Upper riparian animals like hawks and coyotes feed on mid-riparian animals, who feed on water-edge animals. The mid-riparian animals won't survive now, so the bigger animals will forage elsewhere. If this were a federal project, it could never have happened so surreptitiously. It would have required an environmental impact study and public comment, but Oregon's doesn't have a state environmental policy act, so development like this can continue unbridled.

APRIL EIGHTH

Kathie Durbin and photographer Dana Olsen walk with me at Steelman. Now that the shoreline has become readily accessible, we count 13 fire pits in the riparian zone and find many handfuls of fishing line that can strangle birds. I've been making jaunts to observe the damage and read from my journal notes. For example, on Friday, March 27th at 4:30 there were 15 people fishing along the shoreline. Three of them gathered wood and built a fire, which was still smoldering when they left. Sunday, March 29th at 2:30 the parking lot was filled, including eight pickups with horse trailers. In the riparian zone between the parking lot and the lake were 14 horses grazing or being washed, three dogs, nine people and a goat. That same day naturalist Greg Baker had walked along the shore and counted 408 pieces of litter. Dana photographs me as I talk; later I ask him not to print a picture of me with my mouth open. When I repeat this to Mike Houck, he laughs and says they don't make cameras fast enough to get me with my mouth closed.

APRIL ELEVENTH

Kathy Durbin's article begins, "Sauvie Island wildlife watchers are livid…" and it fills a half-page of the Metro section, runs state-wide to more than a third of a million people. I'm thrilled that the editors decided the issue is important enough to give it such significant coverage. My mouth is closed in both photographs.

After the story appears, I receive an offer from two friends with access to heavy equipment, who volunteer to come at night and move boulders to block the boat ramp. Howard proposes, since the new CRMP proposal to prohibit fires is not yet in effect, that we hold a press conference at Steelman, and build 13 bonfires in the fire pits.

APRIL SEVENTEENTH

Disappointed by the horrendous press I've generated, Mike Golden calls early Monday. We set a meeting for today, Friday, to get together over coffee to discuss the issues. In preparation, I spent all day Wednesday organizing my research into a 25-page environmental assessment, supported by 18 pieces of documentation.

My report points out that some of the most basic aspects of a wildlife viewing plan are missing here: there's no objective for the development, public comment wasn't included, and three elemental considerations were ignored—wildlife and their habitat needs, human impacts, and the preferences of wildlife watchers.

On graph paper I've illustrated the size of this parking lot, compared with others I'd measured, and show that it is at least four times as large as necessary or appropriate. Contrasting the site to other wildlife-watching locales, everything about this development becomes questionable, including the trail, the boat ramp and the viewing blinds.

Last night Bob's mother Edith, age 78, died in her sleep. This morning I phone Mike to delay our meeting. Bob's brothers and their wives are flying in to meet us at Edith's home two hours south in Eugene, and I don't know when I'll be back.

APRIL TWENTY-FIFTH

In my mail is a letter dated April 13th from ODFW director Randy Fisher, addressed to the Conservancy and me personally. He writes, "I share your concern for motorized boats launching at the Steelman site. That was not our intent. I have asked that we block the launch."

MAY FIRST

Mike Golden comes over to my office and we talk for an hour and a half. He points out that this was ODFW's first major attempt on the island to meet the needs of wildlife watchers, but he admits that they made some mistakes. Feel free to call me about your concerns, he tells me, with the understanding that I would do so *before* approaching the media. He assures me that despite the contracts, all construction has now been stopped.

JUNE SECOND

Two friends drop by mid-afternoon and drag me from my desk for a short hike at Steelman. I haven't been there in a while because it feels so depressing. What I see makes me angry at myself for not being on guard. Three boulders have been moved to block the boat ramp, but now a six-foot-square cement pad for a kiosk has been constructed near the parking lot, and paths are mowed to the sites of the proposed cement block viewing blinds.

JUNE THIRD

"Mike, I thought you said the construction was stopped," I begin, and describe what I've seen.

"I had the same understanding," he says, "Let me check on this."

He phones later in the day to say the order hadn't been properly communicated to the island's wildlife manager, but that's now taken care of and all further construction is officially halted. We agree that the Conservancy and Portland Audubon will work together with ODFW to create a new plan that will satisfy us all.

JUNE ELEVENTH

A woman friend wants to talk, and we decide to go for a paddle at Steelman. We pick a weekday, late evening of a gray day, hoping not many people will be around. The parking lot is empty. We unload the boats, lift them up over the boulders and carry them down to the water's edge. Since cows no longer graze here, wapato, the wild potato with arrowhead leaves, has appeared along the shore. In the evening quiet my friend says that she's feeling low because she, who desperately wants children, found out that her ex-husband donated his sperm to help his brother's wife have a child. We talk of her sadness, and sense of feeling cheated. Tangerine streaks the sky as we pull into some tall grasses, uncap Blue Heron beers and snack on stone wheat crackers and herb cheese.

It's long past sunset when we get back to the car and load the kayaks. We lift the boats into the saddles on the car rack and tie them in place. In front, in the dark of a starless night, I tie on the bow line with its half hitch knot.

I've learned the ropes.

Chapter 14
Teach the Children Well

Science, throughout my 16 years of schooling, was always a subject to dread. I can still feel the nausea of being forced to slice open a live, wriggling worm with a razor. The acrid smell of formaldehyde anywhere rushes back the memory of dissecting a bulbously swollen frog, its innards dyed blue and red to identify the muscle systems. What wasn't appalling was boring, like memorizing the chart of 105 chemical elements and their symbols: *Be* for beryllium, *Sr* for strontium. Or being tested by rote on the names of rocks I'd never seen. There was no life, or liveliness, in my education of living things.

Then there were the movies.

"I can't believe *you* go camping!" my mother exclaims. "You used to be terrified by a spider."

Like many small-town kids in the '50s, I spent many Sunday afternoons at the matinee, chewing fingernails in fascination and horror as unsuspecting folks were attacked by *The Giant Tarantula* or *The Fly*. Our Catholic school sent us in busloads to watch papal-approved films like *Ben Hur*, where faithful Christians were fed to ravaging lions. I'd have nightmares for weeks over films that are campy laughingstocks today. Wildlife was something to be feared. Who knew when that inky-dinky spider climbing up the waterspout might mutate into a monster.

A few years ago I sat for hours without fear in my kayak as a pod of orca whales played around our boat. At one point a large male, off to our left, its sleek dorsal fin protruding six feet above the surface of the water, headed straight for us, gaining speed. I watched calmly, curiously, knowing from the Whale Museum that orcas had never hurt a human and that if you sit still in your kayak, their echolocation gives them some sense of what you are. Just when it was within striking distance, the whale dove. I peered into the indigo water and watched its massive shape as it swam beneath me, then burst through the surface at a safe distance to my right. Bob had used a hydrophone, an underwater microphone, to record the whales' clicks and conversations. That evening we played back the whale songs, dinner music to the setting sun.

That doesn't mean I've grown fearless. Camping in grizzly bear country, I wore a whistle around my neck and slept with a can of "bear mace" next to my head. But I can look with delight and not terror at a red-sided garter snake slithering in my garden. Or a field mouse, streaking through the living room. Or the bat who's taken up residence for the past three summers in our porch umbrella. I'm learning.

It would be a shame if boredom or fears of ferocious wildlife are bequeathed to children today, especially city kids, because what's left of wildlife habitat is being destroyed quickest of all adjacent to urban areas. If today's kids don't see wildlife, really see, and learn to care, there won't be wildlife for their children and grandchildren.

I once took a workshop entitled "The Ethics of Filmmaking for Children." My notes reflect that there are three ways to teach children about wildlife. Films are the most removed. Experiences brought into the classroom are second. Best of all is to bring children into nature.

Not quite dawn on a Saturday in February, 1991, I'm awakened by the call of a great horned owl, as near as I've ever heard one. This weekend, and for the two weeks following, we're taking care of our godchildren—Sky McKenzie, age 14; Malina, eight, and Jesse, two—while their parents are on vacation. I slip out of bed and tiptoe past the sleeping youngsters to the sliding glass door that opens out back. Excitedly, I realize the owl must be in the old Douglas-fir that we call the Grandfather Tree, adjacent to the house. I listen, then run back and rouse everyone.

"Wake up! Come and hear! There's a great horned owl, hooting! It's the closest I've ever heard one...c'mon!"

Bob sits up in bed, and Sky opens the door to her room. I carry Jesse and groggy Malina. We stand inside in the darkness, Jesse's head on my shoulder, his eyes still closed, listening to the owl's haunting WHO-WHO-Who-who-who. When I slide the door a bit to hear better, the owl stops. The noise must have alarmed it. After a minute the hooting begins again, this time farther away, echoed from deeper in the woods. When we can't hear it anymore, we take turns imitating its WHO-WHO-Who-who-who as we start the pancakes for breakfast.

Sky's friend is going to sleep over, so she and Bob drive into town to pick her up. Malina, Jesse, our new puppy Jibo and I walk over to Virginia Lakes. It's been a dry winter. Usually by early spring the seasonal lakes have water and hundreds of waterfowl, but now the center is marshy, the edges golden with last year's dried grasses. Normally we'd hike on the trail that circles the lake, but the frogs are in full chorus, and Malina asks if we can go down and walk through the dry edge of the lakebed, so that perhaps we might see some.

"What a great idea!" I tell her. I've never walked through the lake before. From down here, the sound of the frog chorus is explosive and thick. Not single notes of *croak* or *rib-it,* but an all-encompassing cloud-like symphony that seems to come from so many directions, it's impossible to know just where to look. Elated, the children steal softly to a particular spot, listen, look at each other, then gleefully giggle. They sneak to another spot. Then another. The frogs are obviously right here, but there's none to be seen.

"Would you like to hear a frog story?" I ask.

"Can I tell one first?" Malina responds.

"Sure."

"Remember when you first moved here, and the little frogs were all over your windows?"

"That was pretty neat, wasn't it?"

"Yeah. They were climbing up the windows, and you could see the little fat pads on their feet."

"Where else were they?"

"Um. They were sleeping on the plant leaves. And we saw that they could change color. The ones on the leaves were green, and the ones on the dirt were brown. And some were hopping around on the grass."

"And do you remember the ones who were nestled at the top of the dining room's sliding glass doors?"

"Yeah, they reminded me of sleeping on bunk beds!…Okay, so what's your frog story?"

"I have a friend, Chris Foster, who lives up on the hill and has a lake. One night there was a full moon and all the frogs were singing, so he and his wife went out to listen. It turned out that all the frogs, maybe a thousand of them, were setting around the edge of the pond. And the moon was so low that it was reflected in the frogs' eyes, so that it looked like the lake was ringed by stars."

"Wow! I'd love to see that sometime!"

"Me, too. Do you know what these little tree frogs are called back East?"

"No, what?"

"Spring peepers."

"Hey! That's a good name because it's almost spring and we're peeping for them!"

When we get back home, it's time for Jesse's nap. They get to choose a children's book from our collection and today they pick *No Star Nights*. It's one of their favorites because it's about little girls in a steel mill town that I've told them looks exactly like Braddock, where I grew up. They point out to me now, "The steel mill looked exactly like that…Your dad looked exactly like that…The nuns looked exactly like that…" The first time an old Pittsburgh friend showed me the book, I opened it and started to cry; sometimes even now I choke up and have to stop reading.

It must seem like a horror book; the children are shocked by the illustrations and can't imagine a place where the sky would glow red at night and no one could see stars. To them, one of the most fascinating pictures is a drawing where the two girls are crouched on the sidewalk in the wind, pulling their skirts down to hide their legs from the graphite that would whip up and sting bare skin like thousands of little knives.

"We did that all the time," I say. The steel mill in the story was shut down, and in the end children look out with their grandfather to the stars. Braddock's is not. I've pasted photographs inside the back cover that I took from my mother's window last year, and they can see how the smoke from the "updated" steel mill obliterates the sky. "Appreciate how beautiful it is here," I always tell them, and I hope that they do.

The story's over, and Jesse knows the nap-time rule: it's okay if he doesn't fall asleep, but he has to stay quietly by himself for one hour. From the living room I can hear him half-whispering to himself and his stuffed rabbit. Then something sounds oddly familiar, and I go and stand hidden behind the doorway. Jesse's crooning himself to sleep, softly calling WHO-WHO-Who-who-who, WHO-WHO-Who-who-who.

Later, in April, we take Jesse and Malina on an Audubon birdwatching trip to a rookery of great blue herons, where we hope to see newborns in their nests. Sky, in her second year of teendom, would rather spend the weekend at her friend's house.

This rookery adjoins the Heron Lakes golf course, and the group of a dozen and a half binocular-clad birdwatchers waits for Mike Houck's signal before crossing over the manicured grasses. Even though it's only 7:30 in the morning, golfers are already driving the greens and Mike urges everyone to move quickly so we don't disturb their play. Bob carries Jesse and I scurry Malina along. She insists on carrying our spotting scope, and has it slung over her shoulder in imitation of Houck.

"I can set up the scope," Malina brags. "Remember I did it when we saw the goldfinches?"

"Go ahead," Bob tells her. "Can you see the nests?"

"No."

"Here, take the binoculars and look up in the trees. The heron nests are big platforms of twigs and pretty easy to spot. See how many you can count."

"Oh, I see one. Oh! Let's see...hmmm...I count nine." Now she's befuddled. "Where should I point the scope?"

"Do you see any babies sticking out of any of the nests?"

"Let me look, too," Jesse says as Bob hands him the small pair of binoculars we've brought for him, and helps him to focus.

"No, I don't see any babies," Malina says.

"Let's go see where Mike has his scopes pointed. Maybe he's found some."

Sure enough, the Audubon scopes are aimed at a nest with three young herons, waving their javelin-like beaks in the air, on the lookout for food-bearing parents.

Malina waits in line to look through the big scopes.

"Do you see the babies?" Bob asks.

"Yeah! I see...three!"

"What do they look like?"

"Oh, gosh. The hair on the top of their heads is sticking straight up! They look like punk rock birds! How cool!"

She moves aside to let the next person in line have a look and figures out where to set up our scope.

"I'm going to make it low so Jesse and I can look," she explains.

"That's fine. Donna and I can watch with our binoculars."

"Here, Jesse," Malina holds his head so his eye looks through the lens. "See the baby birds? Look at their silly hair!"

Bob, who's scanning the sky and treetops, calls out, "Here comes a parent bringing food. Watch this!"

"Is that the mom or dad?"

"I don't know. Both heron parents feed the babies and they look alike."

"Hey, the babies are stabbing the parent!" Malina yells as the young all jump up, trying to grab the parent's beak with their own. "What are they feeding those babies?"

"The parents get things like fish or frogs or mice and chew them up, then spit them in the baby's mouth," I tell her.

"Gross!"

"Maybe that same kind of stuff is in kids' baby food. It's always soft and squishy," I tease.

"No way!" Malina retorts.

Eventually we spot young great blue herons in most of the nests, and spend another hour watching the parents fly in to feed them. Each time the crowd yells and points, giving a chew-by-chew description:

Which baby got the morsel. Or it fell out of the parent's mouth, and now they're all squabbling over it. Or two babies are having a tug-of-war, pulling it between their beaks.

How long before the babies can fly on their own?" Malina asks.

"About two months," I tell her. "Would you want to come back and watch when they're learning to fly?"

"Oh, yeah!"

Scopes folded, the crowd waits for a foursome to finish a hole, then scuttles past. When we get back to the car, Malina reaches into her pocket and pulls out a golf ball.

"Look what I found!"

Jesse, now four, is laughing hysterically at himself in the mirror, dressed for kayaking in my long underwear held up with a belt.

"It's kind of a Teenage Mutant Ninja Turtle outfit, don't you think?" I ask encouragingly, hoping he won't refuse to go out in such ridiculous attire.

I should have recognized their excitement and not worried. It's two years later, February, 1993, and our godchildren's parents left on another well-deserved vacation, and Jesse and Malina, now ten, are staying with us. Sky, age 16 and newly-earned driver's license in hand, opted to stay in town with her aunt. Today is the kids' first sea kayak trip.

Cotton clothes wouldn't do, because when they're wet, they draw on the body's warmth to make you colder. So yesterday evening I'd dragged out my wool and polypropylene clothes and piled them in stacks: Long underwear tops. Bottoms. Socks. Gloves. Hats. Scarves. Jackets. We gathered binoculars, field guides, thermos bottles, camera and camp seats, then baked chocolate chip cookies.

When Marcia Hoyt arrives, Jesse and Malina, absurdly wrapped in layers of outsize clothes, slip on their new rubber boots. Bob has gone to Howard's to help him load his three-seater kayak we're borrowing, a Sisyutl, named after the fearsome double-headed sea serpent of northwest coastal Indian legend.

Steelman Lake is frozen, and Howard throws a few rocks, then judges from the sound that we won't be able to break through the ice in our kayaks. Even though there's a string of clear water, Howard points out that even if we made it around, we'd never be able to get through the Narrows, which is the most protected part of the lakes and would have the thickest ice. I recall that last year there was ice in the Narrows when it was nowhere else and agree. We pile in the cars and drive to the Oak Island put-in.

Marcia takes her place in the Sisyutl's front seat, Malina holding the puppy Jibo in the center, and Jesse and I in the rear. Even though I'd rearranged the foot pedals so I could reach them, with Jesse on my lap I can't move my legs and decide I'll have to steer with paddle strokes instead of the rudder, a much more difficult arrangement in a barge like the Sisyutl.

Howard and Bob give us all a shove and we're afloat. Swans fly overhead and I suggest we start to make a count of all the birds we see. A bald eagle. Another eagle. Ducks, 35, 36, 37. Geese, add 42. By the time we paddle to the other side of the lake, we've spotted more than 1,100 ducks and geese, 27 swans and 14 bald eagles.

The shoreline is muddy, and the kids are hesitant to get out. "That's why you're wearing those rubber boots," I remind them. "Your feet won't get wet. Go ahead and stomp around in the mud."

"Hey, this is fun!" Jesse exclaims as he splashes through small pools of water.

"Kids, come and look at this," Marcia calls. She shows them where a beaver has chewed the bark of a tree. "Here, put your fingers in the grooves. Can you feel that? Those are the marks from the beaver's teeth."

Jesse and Malina, chocolate chip cookies in hand, rub the gnawed wood with their fingertips and closely inspect the wave-like patterns.

Howard looks up at the sky and cautions, "Those are mighty dark clouds over the Tualatins. It's doing something up there." As soon as he finishes his sentence, a few snowflakes begin to fall and we notice the temperature has dropped.

"Are you cold?" I ask the kids, and Malina bashfully nods yes. "I think Marcia and I ought to take the kids back," I tell Bob and Howard. "We can't paddle that fast, so you'll catch up with us before the take-out."

By now it's snowing heartily and the far reaches of the lake are becoming obliterated from view by the falling flakes. The water is slate gray and getting a bit roily from the wind, so the boat rocks. I notice that when I use a sweep stroke, the force of it splashes water onto Jesse, and his paddle jacket is soaking wet. It's waterproof and I'm thankful I made them wear the right clothes. Taking out my binoculars, I scan the far shoreline to see where our cars are parked.

Marcia and I are paddling hard, and that's keeping us warm, but I imagine the children are starting to chill. Jesse's face burns, he's frightened, and he starts to cry. At first I'd tried to stay chipper, so the children won't be worried, but now I see a more drastic enthusiasm is needed.

"We're paddling in the snow, we're paddling in the snow," I start to sing at my loudest and cheeriest, to the tune of "Singing in the Rain." "What a glorious feeling, we're happy again." Marcia pipes in, then we lose track of the words and verses.

"What would you like to sing, Malina?" Marcia asks.

"Rudolph," she says, and starts leading us in her version of "Rudolf the Red-Nosed Reindeer." Jesse has stopped crying and I re-wrap the scarf around his ruddy face.

As we paddle closer to shore, the snow falls harder. Frozen crystals sting our faces. By now Howard and Bob, concerned about the weather, have caught up.

"Are you the leader?" Jesse asks Howard.

"I guess so," Howard answers.

"You're a good leader," Jesse tells him.

In soft phases, the ghostly shoreline takes shape as we approach. All the branches of the trees, the rocks, and the ground are coated with a frosting of snow.

When we finally land, I want to jump out of the kayak and get the kids warm, but instead of pulling us in, Howard and Bob are standing and laughing at us and Bob insists on taking our picture. The wind has blown the snow from the left, and there we sit lined up in the kayak, with only the left side of our hats and coats caked white with snow.

Later, when the children are toasty from dry clothes and hot chocolate, we asked them if they would ever go kayaking again.

"Not when it's snowing!" Jesse exclaims.

The following weekend Bob has to work, so I give the kids a choice.

"We can go to Virginia Lakes, or go hiking up in the hills at Howard's or we can borrow his Sisyutl again and go kayaking.

To my surprise, without hesitation, they both agree, "Let's go kayaking!"

"But this time," Malina adds, "I want to paddle."

Malina confidently settles herself in the front seat of the boat, and turns around. "Last time, I didn't tell you this, but I was scared when we started out. Now I'm not scared any more."

"I can tell," I assure her.

She catches on quickly to the rudiments of paddling but the lake is so shallow that unless we pay attention, our paddles scrape the bottom and bring up globs of mud. Howard pulls alongside and explains how the aerodynamics of the shallow water slows our boats, and shows us how to paddle efficiently across the water's surface.

"I hear a kingfisher," Malina states with certainty. I look around, but I've never seen kingfishers on the lake. "There!" she points jubilantly, to a kingfisher sitting on a branch just ahead of us. "I recognized it from those bird tapes we've been playing when you drive us to school in the mornings." Then she proudly turns around and paddles with vigor.

"You're getting to be a really great spotter," I tell her, rather amazed myself.

Since Jesse's seated in the middle seat he can't see ahead, so every bird that flies overhead he hollers, "What's that bird?"

"It's a hawk. I'm not sure which kind. You can tell it's a hawk and not a vulture because its wings are straight out. A vulture flies with its wings in a V. That's how you can remember it—V is for vulture."

"What's *that* bird?"

"That a gull. It's flying low looking for fish to eat."

"What are those two white birds?"

"Those are swans. Aren't they beautiful?"

By the time we pull back ashore, Malina has spotted another kingfisher, a bald eagle, and a flock of sandhill cranes.

"Why can't you make the crane sound?" she asks me.

"I don't know," I say and try fruitlessly again, my tongue sticking as usual to the roof of my mouth.

"I can," she reminds me as she vibrates her tongue into an excellent imitation of the cranes' familiar rolling *r*. "Too bad we're not going to be here for any more weekends. But next time we come out, will you take me kayaking?"

"Me, too?" Jesse echoes.

"Of course."

"Howard, will you be the leader again?" Jesse asks.

"Of course," he answers with a smile. "Will you be big enough then to help me lift this boat?"

We've been romanticizing about moonlight hikes. Tonight is the full moon, and the last night of the children's stay.

"Can we go out hiking tonight?" Malina asks.

"Sure, why not?" I say.

We bundle up and walk, without a flashlight, through our woods. The frogs from the lake of the adjoining farm are in full chorus and the moon casts perfect shadows through bare branches across the winding overgrown path. In one place, a number of trees have fallen from the winter storms and the open area is brilliant with light.

"Look!" Jesse exclaim. "There's a ring around the moon."

Malina and I look up to see the rainbow glow that perfectly encircles the moon.

"I wonder if that's a parhelion," I muse.

"What's that?" Malina asks.

"A parhelion is a halo like that around the sun. But *helios* means sun. So is a halo around the moon called a par*lun*ion, because *luna* is moon? What do you think?"

"I don't know."

"So, do you think it's *loony* to be out walking in the moonlight?"

"No way!" she exclaims.

"No way!" Jesse echoes. "Listen. I think I hear the owl!"

Chapter 15
Shadow Limbs

As I pore through the pages of the C3-93 Staff Report from the Multnomah County Division of Planning and Development entitled "West Hills Study Area Scenic Resources/Determination of Significance," I am outraged. Enraged. Furious. Livid. Rabid. Wild. My father's Italian profanities burst from repressed memory past my normally genteel lips. I quake. Thunder. Seethe.

The county planning report, prepared for the July 26, 1993 Planning Commission Hearing, concludes that "The West Hills, the landform consisting of the front of the Tualatin Mountains, are not an outstanding scenic resource" and thus are not required to be included in Goal 5's environmental protection program. So, my beloved and beautiful Tualatin Mountains have no significant scenic values? This report just clears the way, doesn't it? It just clears the way for the horrendous proposed freeway to go ripping through. For that hideous quarry to gouge out more of the forests. For added acres of clearcuts that strip away trees and sprout glaring white mega-mansions along the mountain crest.

Oh, I'm madder than a hornet. My blood's boiling. I'm fit to be tied. And I know that this is good.

The emerging field of ecopsychology aims to revamp our definition of mental health. Sanity, according to its proponents, includes a healthy relationship with nature, as well as with our parents, partners and siblings. Dysfunction in our urban technological lives—depression, neuroses and other disorders—might be diagnosed as our dissociation from the earth, and the deep psychological wounds of living on a planet where species by the day are becoming extinct.

As a result, people in our culture often suffer from what Robert Lifton describes as "psychic numbing." The magnitude of threats to the earth and all its creatures can feel so overwhelming that the tendency is to repress our awareness of the environment, to render it unconscious. In so doing, we stifle our openness to joy and pleasure, we anesthetize our senses and disown our innate life forces.

What is the alternative? To feel the pain, the grief, the guilt of assaulting the place where we live? Well, yes. That's the first step to healing. Pain and sadness are an acknowledgment that we care, that we feel interconnected to the earth beyond our human bodies. In her essay, "Working through Environmental Despair" in the book *Ecopsychology*, Joanna Macy uses the metaphor "shadow limb." She writes, "Just as an amputee continues to feel twinges in the severed limb, so in a sense do we experience, in anguish for homeless people or hunted whales, pain that belongs to a separated part of our body—a larger body than we thought we had, unbounded by our skin."

For the most sensitive of us, shadow limbs twinge daily. Just this morning a front page headline blared, "House GOP upends Endangered Species Act." While many people might flip the page in a deadened hopelessness, others will allow themselves to feel their outrage, and will sharpen their consciousness and move to act on behalf of all wildlife and habitat.

So I come to understand that my anger is a normal, mentally healthy, natural response to the degradation of a place I love. Responding to that anger, working to protect the mountains, helps me find harmony within.

One of Oregon's enviable land use laws is State Goal 5, which requires jurisdictions to "conserve open space and protect natural and scenic resources." Multnomah County has been ordered to determine whether the Tualatin Mountains have significant Goal 5 resources in four categories: Wildlife, Streams, Scenic, and Aggregate. Portland Audubon and Friends of Forest Park are coordinating research from wildlife biologists, geologists, hydrologists, wetland experts and attorneys to address Wildlife, Streams and Aggregate. It falls on the Sauvie Island Conservancy, since the mountains are the backdrop for the entire island, to tackle the realm of Scenic.

Like the sensual velvety folds of a theater curtain, the 900- to 1,500-foot Tualatin Mountains grace the stage of everything we do outdoors on the island, and many lovely places beyond. Turning a bend on a bicycle, I'm awed as their coniferous and deciduous forests fill my frame of vision, vine maples in autumn cloaked in persimmon and fiery red. From the lakes, the gentle undulating range forms a spectacular miles-long panorama. On Bald Eagle Watches we spend hours scanning the forested mountaintops for the raptors to emerge from their roosts. My favorite drives are up the Tualatins' steep and narrow winding woodland roads, probably not much different from the wagon routes of their names today—Cornelius Pass, Rocky Point and Logie Trail.

Are these the same mountains described in C3-93? It says perfunctorily, "There is little variety in the landform, being fairly uniform in height and appearance…From Highway 30, there is little scenic integrity…When viewed from a distance, the modifications caused by logging are very apparent…The BPA power line is very visible…There are no recognized public points where the public goes specifically to view the West Hills…The lack of safe places to stop [along the Sauvie Island roads] makes these roads of limited value as viewpoints…Compared to other scenic areas of the county, like the Columbia Gorge, the mountains "do not possess the scenic qualities to be considered outstanding."

Chris Wrench, president of Friends of Forest Park, phones with some assistance. "We found an expert, Richard Shaffer, who's offered to help us *pro bono* if we just cover his expenses. He's retired now, but he was the principal landscape architect for Mount Hood National Forest for 23 years. Let's set up a time to show him the mountains."

Minutes after we're introduced, even before a tour of the Tualatins, Richard begins to offer scathing rebuttal of the report. "The comparison with the Columbia River Gorge is incorrect and unfair. The Gorge is a National Scenic Area, but if you used this report's methodology, you can say that, for example, the Columbia Gorge isn't scenic compared to the Grand Canyon." He's doubly miffed because he disagrees with a lot of the report's basic criteria, yet of the five sources listed in the planner's Bibliography, two are documents that Richard authored for Mount Hood.

We drive down Sauvie Island Road and as he photographs the mountain forests across the channel, Richard notes that some of the more recent clearcuts already have trees six feet tall and even the newest clearcuts are layered in shades of green. Walks to Hadley's Landing, Virginia Lakes, Coon Point and the Bybee-Howell House are clear evidence of public places where the mountains dominate the view. He even takes a photo of the non-official "eagle viewing area." When he leaves, he drives alone to Kelley Point, a city park on the mainland beyond the island across the Willamette River, to see how the mountains crown the landscape, even from there.

Although I enjoyed the outing with Richard and Chris, I'm piqued that I had to take a whole afternoon from work and am still writing in my office at nine at night, all because of the—to me—earth-blindness of the planning report.

"Scenic values probably aren't as important as wildlife or streams," I say to a psychiatrist acquaintance, perhaps too apologetically, as I describe these issues.

"Don't underestimate the value of scenic beauty in our lives," he interjects. "For example, one of the tools that therapists use to help people alleviate stress is called 'creative visualization.' What kind of places do you think people imagine when they want to feel calm and serene? It's always places of scenic beauty, like waterfalls, and forests and mountains.

"And here's another side to that: every time I drive into town on Sunset Highway on a clear day, I have a psychological trauma."

I know what he's talking about and smile cynically, "Because the KOIN tower blocks the view of Mount Hood."

"I loved that view. For years, I'd drive through the tunnel and there was the mountain. It was magnificent. And now the view is gone. It still upsets me."

"Did you know," I sympathize, "that so many people were angry about that view being destroyed, that's one of the reasons the city of Portland developed a Scenic Resources Plan? And do you know they determined the most important scenic views to protect? They took nominations from something like 400 neighborhood associations, interest groups and all kinds of people."

"But you're telling me this county plan was written without input from citizens at all?

"No one asked us."

C3-93 goes before the nine-member Planning Commission of unpaid appointed citizens. They must decide whether to accept this Staff Report, but we hope they will lean on the side of the environment and scenic values and reject it. I have organized people to testify: Richard Shaffer; Jim Sjulin, who works for Portland Parks; Conservancy members Jerome DeGraaff and Jack Sanders, who's videotaped the mountains from the air; attorney Neil Kagan; and Arnie Rochlin of Friends of Forest Park.

As the commission discusses the report, I'm stunned. Flabbergasted. Infuriated. One commissioner comments, "Viewing is so subjective it gets into problems that become big hassles." Another remarks, "I'm not convinced that people look up to those mountains. I know how much bicyclists and runners do and don't because they're my friends." The commission adopted the Findings and Conclusions of the Staff Report, recommending that the Board of County Commissioners not designate the West Hills Scenic Study Area a significant scenic resource.

In ecopsychology, therapists have pondered what happens to the psyche when people return from extended time in the wilderness. Within days, hours sometimes, people are often enveloped in depression and despair. It's culture shock, but the culture is our own. This has led to an exploration of ways to continue the connection with wilderness in daily urban life. I liken this psychospiritual dysfunction to the despair we feel at our defeats in politics for the environment. The question is the same: how do we restore our damaged psyches? Some of the ecopsychologists' suggestions include meditation, earth restoration work, developing rituals, or connecting regularly with groups. The one I find most important for myself is Ritual.

Every morning I have a ritual that takes just a few minutes but reconnects me with the earth and revives my spirits, no matter how trying the time. It's the act of filling the bird feeders. Depending on the time of year, I might have as many as a dozen birdfeeders plus a 14-foot-long, six-inch-wide fence board that I heap with food. Some days I scrub out the bird baths and replenish them with fresh water. Regardless of weather, I'm out there, without jacket or hat, in clogs without socks, to feel the day.

I don't treat it like any other chore; I'm mindful of the experience. Scooping the seeds, smoothing my fingers over the hand-made wooden feeders, listening to birds chatter as they wait in the limbs above, smelling the scents of the season, noticing flowers or berries in bloom, consciously appreciating how I nurture these wild creatures who live in or pass through our yard.

For even the most skyscraper-bound city dweller, small daily rituals—a detour through a park, attentively tending a plant—can keep us in touch with the earth, and keep us sane.

The next stage in the saga of C3-93 is an October 12th public hearing before the Board of County Commissioners, five elected officials who have the final vote. We've brought even more people to testify on behalf of the scenic beauty of the mountains. I say this:

> The Conservancy concurs with Richard Shaffer's
> report, which points out that the Staff Report
> is "technically invalid, uses erroneous inventory
> criteria, suspect rationale and incorrect and unfair
> comparisons."

I'm stunned by the Planning Memorandum attached to today's Hearing Report that says Multnomah Channel and Sauvie Island weren't taken into consideration. That means the scenic values for the Tualatin Mountains would be determined without considering where they're seen *from?* Could this be more ludicrous?

I lead canoe, kayak and bicycle trips for Portland Audubon and Portland Parks on Sauvie Island and I can assure you that not only are people looking at the mountains, they're looking at them from four to eight hours on these outdoor excursions.

The light in our area is muted light, which is like the soft filter that Hollywood directors use to hide the wrinkles of aging actors. In the same way, where these mountains have been logged, they don't have garish clearcuts, but most often look like undulating folds in various shades of green velvet.

The Staff Report totally ignores the beauty of the mountains and their importance to the scenic views of Sauvie Island and the Willamette River Greenway. The report also ignores the remarkable nature of having such a green panorama on the very outskirts of downtown Portland—a panorama that would be the envy of any other city.

The timbre of the Board of Commissioners is very different from the Planning Commission. Immediately Dan Saltzman, the commissioner representing our area, makes a motion to declare the mountains a "significant scenic resource."

He goes on to explain, "I don't agree that because we have other scenic views that's reason to penalize those who appreciate the Tualatin Mountains. And I don't buy into the logic that we have enough designated areas. The mountains are an integral part of the framework of views from these other places."

In seconding the motion, commissioner Sharron Kelley says, "I view the information presented by staff as not relevant to the debate. In competition with local resources, the mountains are outstanding."

Concurring, commissioner Gary Hansen points out, "This is a beautiful scenic area. Our duty as county commissioners is clearly to protect this type of resource."

Commission chair Beverly Stein comments, "As pointed out by Mr. Shaffer, it's not fair to compare these mountains to the Columbia Gorge. And traveling along the roads should be considered. These mountains are a backdrop for our lives that we would miss if they weren't there."

The county commissioners vote unanimously to declare the mountains a significant scenic resource. In giving direction to the planner to rewrite the report, Beverly adds, "…and if there's some way to keep those undulating folds of velvet…" Unanimously, the motion carries.

C3-93a, the new staff report, includes an ESEE (Economic, Social, Environmental and Energy) analysis and new Findings and Conclusions. In it, the mountains have significant scenic values and are described much differently: "Various canyons bisect the face of the range, adding variety to landform… Logging activity has created variety in the vegetative pattern, with different ages of regrowth appearing as different textures and shades of green…The mountains cannot be fairly compared to other recognized scenic areas in the county; they are a different landscape character…"

There are a few addition to the document I particularly savor:

"The West Hills also have a psychological value to some people, being perceived as an integral and important part of the forested landscape linking Forest Park to the Coast Range, and contributing to the image of a natural area on the outskirts of a city."

And, finally: "The hills are an integral part of the scenic framework of Sauvie Island, the Multnomah Channel, and the Willamette River… When viewed from a distance, such as the Sauvie Island Wildlife Area, the hills appear to be a velvety green background…"

Chapter 16
Earth Sisters

On my birthday she gave me a card covered with a watercolor painting of striped and polka-dotted tulips, and around the printed greeting she wrote, "The bond that links your true family is not one of blood, but of respect and joy in each others' lives. Rarely do members of one family grow up under the same roof. I love you. Mary Rose (p.s. the quote is from Richard Bach)." Today we're crowded in a small fitting room and I'm zipping her into an off-the-shoulder white sheath hemmed in ornate lace, a stunning wedding dress possibility. With her mother and two sisters still living in their Indiana hometown, I am family.

Mary Rose and I became close the summer she moved to Portland after college, to take a landscape architect job with Murase Associates, the firm that loaned FAUNA meeting space. She hung around and involved herself in our work. Old enough to be her mother, and an embarrassingly sluggish bicyclist, I was looking for a rider to help me train for Cycle Oregon, an annual weeklong, 500-mile jaunt across the state's back roads. That year the route would cross four mountain passes. Mary Rose could easily outpace me, but she was looking for a friend and held back her strength. So we spent long hot Saturdays cycling languidly around charmingly-named routes like Tile Flats, Grabhorn, Verboort, and Champoeg, working up to 65-, then 75- mile days, stopping on our way home for beers and tortilla chips.

We often talked about her swift disillusionment with landscape architecture, and her longing to do something more significant for the earth. When Mike Houck told her of a graduate assistantship in Portland State University's School of Urban Affairs, she applied and quit her job within the hour her acceptance letter arrived. For two years she struggled through the masters program, but when it was over, didn't hunt for a well-paying government job. Instead, she became the community organizer for a small local environmental group, Friends of Trees, and works with people in neighborhoods to coordinate street tree plantings. Her satisfaction comes not only from helping neighbor meet neighbor and bringing nature to their streets. She finds the most rewarding part the Youth Tree Corps, where she helps high school students tackle the responsibility of coordinating their own tree plantings. I delight in her daily joy at having work so totally and purely helping society and the environment.

After trying on half a dozen gowns, she suggests we head to Torrefazione Cafe, knowing my idea of "Shop 'til you drop" is a maximum of one hour in stores of any sort.

"Ever have a granita?" Mary Rose asks. "It's my favorite." I follow her advice and am immediately hooked on what tastes like a slushy coffee fudgesicle. We couple that with crusty Italian rolls.

"Remember the first time Bob and I met Ron?" I reminisce with her. "You brought him to Thanksgiving dinner. I was fond of him right away. It made me smile that he was so nervous about meeting us. I thought his caring that much was really sweet, and a sign of something good."

More than two years after its first failed attempt, the Greenspaces bond measure is going back on the ballot, in November, 1995. It's a little different this time, a $135,600,000 bond measure that identifies 6,000 acres of natural areas to be purchased, instead of a $200,000,000 blank check. Tonight the Resolution that initiates the campaign will be voted on by the Metro Council. Seated on either side of me in Metro's hearing chamber are Richard Meyer, who's the director of Portland Audubon, and Ron Carley, Mary Rose's sweetheart, who's their outreach coordinator. We've had to wait five hours to testify, because the councilors did not limit testimony to the usual three minutes. One small-town mayor was allowed to rant for an hour how they didn't need any more land taken off the tax rolls. Many of the other environmentalists have left.

On Richard's leather-gloved hand is Dots the Pygmy Owl, a permanently wounded bird who lives at Audubon's Wildlife Care Center, and he warns me not to lean too close. Even though she's only six inches tall, her talons can rip apart a chicken. When Richard at last gets to the microphone, he explains why he brought Dots: because wildlife adds excitement to our lives, and wild creatures and their habitat connect our spirits to nature. I notice that as he talks, Dots poops on the new Metro carpeting.

After all the testimony there's a ten-minute break before the council votes, and I'm ready to head home. "You can't leave!" Richard protests. Ron adds, "We've got to see this ourselves and celebrate. Come with us for a drink." We rush over to a bar next door where Ron and Richard each drink double Wild Turkeys and I gulp down a glass of red wine. Quickly returning, we giggle irreverently in the back as the "yes" count is unanimous, give each other high-fives, and vow that this time we'll make sure we win, because we know it's the last chance.

"What are you doing for the next six months?" John Sherman calls to ask.

"What's up?"

"We've got a donor who's offered to give $10,000 to the Greenspaces campaign. Richard Meyer and I talked about using the money to hire a grassroots coordinator. And, we think it should be you. So, will you do it and can you start right away?"

"John, there are lots of other people who could do that better than me. Besides, it's October and I've committed to writing projects through December."

"Name me somebody."

"Well, I can't come up with anyone off the top of my head."

"There you have it. Think it over and call me back."

Like a spineless, continually shape-changing amoeba, a loose campaign group begins to form. When a Steering Committee becomes official, I'm excited to be one of the fifteen chosen, which promptly becomes meaningless. Whoever is dedicated enough to show up every two weeks and take on a task becomes an integral part.

We're a cheery, high-spirited lot, except for Patricia McCaig, a new Metro councilor. She runs the meetings with mercilessly serious speed, threatens to kick out anyone who hasn't done a task they've committed to, and announces at least once each gathering, "You're all going to hate me by the time this is over." John keeps reminding me how fortunate we are to have her committed to our cause; a few years earlier she ran the successful campaign to elect Barbara Roberts, Oregon's first woman governor, and became even more politically well-connected as Roberts' chief of staff.

First orders of business are to raise money and hire a campaign manager. The personification of our collective list of criteria includes: Experience running campaigns. Knowledgeable about grassroots organizing. Passion for wildlife. Sense of fun. Energy. Creativity. Superb organizer. Ability to embrace others' ideas. Heart.

Patricia recommends her friend Liz Kaufman to be hired as fundraiser. "She's tireless and relentless and you'll hate her by the end of the campaign" are Patricia's selling points. We have no money actually in the bank, and Liz proposes to raise $25,000 in a month. She's in.

Ron had taken a workshop called "Running a Movement Campaign" that Liz taught at a community organizing conference. He thinks she's terrific, and recommends her as campaign manager. For that position, Liz proposes combining forces with Gene Duvernoy, who had run a similar campaign in Seattle. The Steering Committee sends a Request For Quotes to eighteen potential campaign managers, and Gene and Liz get the job.

Our delightful time two years ago with the Birdhouse in the Square gets me dreaming about more whimsical wildlife schemes to reach voters. We could take Dots and Syd the Red-tailed Hawk to shopping malls. Have children paint wildlife murals, which would go on campaign flyers. Inspire artists to create giant flora and fauna costumes—hemlock trees and great blue herons—for us to wear passing out brochures. Schedule Wildlife Walk parades, with fabric-art wetlands and forests studded with costumed creatures. I fill a journal with scribbled drawings and notes.

Soon I realize this campaign won't waste a minute on such well-meaning frivolity. It's numbers, numbers, numbers. Yet listening to them, I can hear the rumbles of victory, and I'm drawn down their path.

The campaign strategy appears simple: There are 750,000 registered voters in Multnomah County. Measure 26-26, as it has been named, will be a special election mail-in ballot, which has never had a voter turnout of more than 37 percent. So even at forty percent, that's 300,000 votes. To win, Liz continually reminds us, we need 150,000 votes plus one. The last Greenspaces measure was included in a general election with an 85 percent turnout. Even though we lost, the final count showed that 233,399 people voted "yes" for greenspaces. All we need to do is find 150,001 of them, and make sure they mail in their ballots.

Liz and Gene anticipate it will cost at least $250,000 to accomplish this, and within two months, aided by Patricia and John, they've already raised $60,000. Once the strategy is approved by the Steering Committee, Gene steps aside and Liz runs the show.

Bob encouraged me and I made up my mind that I would accept John's grassroots organizing position if it were officially offered to me. But one of Liz's first decisions is to hire three young, campaign-savvy women as field organizers, and another as publicity coordinator. I'm disappointed but secretly relieved, and then excited as Caroline Fitchett, Terry Horton, Aisling Coghlan and Dawn Del Rio bedazzle us all with their commitment and long, long hours.

The problem, though, is that they don't know the local conservation activists. People who put in months of work on the last campaign are offended when the field organizers call them as potential volunteers, and of course, never heard of them.

A drizzly Sunday Mary Rose and I hike with Jibo in Forest Park along a cascading creek, sharing our concerns about how to connect the campaign staff with all the FAUNA and Audubon environmentalists who might be willing to help. Beneath the towering cedars and cottonwoods, our boots softly sinking in the mossy trail, we come up with the idea of having the more well-known FAUNA leaders call each group's contact person, introduce the campaign staff, and ask for their involvement. Ten of us make 140 phone calls, and roll the activists into action.

Volunteers offer varying degrees of commitment. But a core group of devotees, including Mary Rose, Ron and I, become the field organizers' virtual slaves: ask us; we'll do it.

"You need an ink jet printer? Hey, my friend Jan tried to sell hers to me. It's still sitting in my office. Maybe she'll donate it for a writeoff." Two days later: "Bob will drop it by."

"Speak at a fund-raising coffee? Sure. When is that?"

"A guy wants to make a video for cable TV? You'd like me to be there when you meet with him? When's he coming?"

"Critique the slide show you put together? Okay." Later: "Liz, you need more wildlife slides. Ask Ron Klein for his shots. Especially include that cute frog."

"Speak at some neighborhood meetings? I'll do that. You'll FAX me a list?" Later: "I'll commit to one a week. I've marked Reed Neighborhood Association and Woodstock Community Center for the next two weeks. You'll FAX me directions? I should pick up the slides at six?"

"Write a few Letters to the Editor? Yeah, I could find the time. I'll write a sample and let Dawn check it over."

"Oh, no! Paid radio ads are bashing Metro? You'd like me to call in on Bill Gallagher's radio talk show? His whole show will be about the bond measure? What time? Do you have that station number?"

"Will you have some brochures and a sign-up sheet ready for me to take to our kayak club meeting?" Later: "Liz, what did you want me to see? Inside the new brochure? Oh, you included the frog shot, full page! It's fabulous! You're laughing. Of course, you knew I'd love it!"

"Will I call all my friends who I think are "yes" votes and get them to confirm that? Well, if I called people I'd end up yakking for hours. How about if I do a mailing instead?"

"I'm going to the Green City Data students' presentation day. Give me a few hundred flyers and I'll ask the kids to pass them out in their neighborhoods."

Endorsements are rolling in: Home Builders Association, Gray Panthers, *The Oregonian,* Portland Association of Teachers, *The Business Journal,* Beaverton Chamber of Commerce, League of Women Voters, Willamette Pedestrian Coalition. The campaign letterhead now lists more than three dozen organizations in support. $200,000 have been raised and the goal is upped to $300,000. We are all swept up in the possibility, the probability, of actually winning.

Election day is May 16th, and door-to-door canvassing weekends are set for March 11th, April 8th, 22nd and 29th. The most enthusiastic campaigners have been named "captains" and we've each organized a team of volunteers. Sauvie Island Conservancy members were so eager to help that our team has nearly twenty canvassers.

I coaxed my goddaughter Malina into joining us, and Saturday morning we pack bags of snacks for our team, then meet to carpool with Stu Sandler and Beth Gibans beneath the island bridge. We meet up with the rest at our "training session," held in a conference room at the Hallmark Inn. We'd hardly needed to bring extra food, as people are already snacking on the coffee, juice, fruits, bagels and muffins I didn't realize would be provided.

"I'm thrilled to see so many of you show up in the rain," Terry welcomes us. "Actually, the rain makes your job easier, because people realize you're really committed, and they listen a lot more." She hands out scripts and we practice knocking on doors and addressing potential voters before heading out.

Malina and I select a neighborhood from a box of homemade clipboards. Each holds a map of twenty or so streets, a pen, street-by-street computer printouts that the campaign has purchased which list regular voters of mail-in elections, all covered with a sheet of plastic to stay dry. Then we take a stack of flyers that show specific greenspaces in that area likely to be purchased if the bond measure passes.

It rains on and off as we walk the streets of Hillsboro, a suburban enclave of small houses with neat lawns and borders of tulips and daffodils, children's tricycles and basketball hoops crowding driveways. Malina doesn't want to speak, so we develop a routine: she rings the doorbell, I give the spiel, and then she hands the person the flyers. By the end of our three hours, we haven't finished all the streets on our list, but it's time to return to the meeting spot. We tally our votes: 17 "Yes," three "No" and five "Maybe."

When Malina's dad comes to pick her up that night and asks how it went, she surprises me by saying, "You pretend you're living in the house and I knock on the door." "Okay," he says. And Malina proceeds to give her version of my presentation: "Are you Mike McKenzie? I'm Malina McKenzie and we're here today volunteering for Yes on 26-26. Do you know about this bond measure? ..." It dawns on me that I had not imagined the kind of lesson she learned.

When I phone Liz Monday to see how the canvassing went region-wide, she reports that almost 400 volunteers went door-to-door and talked to over 10,000 voters. I'm exuberant; Liz is subdued. This was the first big push of the campaign and no one, I think, but Ron, Mary Rose, Richard and I imagined we could bring out this many volunteers. Now I can't fathom how we could lose. "It's my job to be negative," Liz explains, but I am utterly optimistic just the same.

Mom has come to visit from Braddock for two weeks, and I plan things for her to share with my extended family here. Saturday night Ron and Mary Rose, Ali Highberger and her boyfriend Dan Weig and a dozen others join us for a potluck dinner and Bob and I show slides of our January cross-country ski trip to Yellowstone. Even with our little point-and-shoot Nikon, the close-ups of bison on the trail, elk along the rivers, hot springs, geysers, mudpots and mountain panoramas draw gasps from this outdoorsy crowd.

Tuesday we meet Mary Rose for lunch. The wedding gown she ordered has arrived and she models it for Mom, who is as enthralled and proud as if it were her own daughter's. From the bridal shop the gown is entrusted to me so Ron doesn't accidentally or intentionally come upon it. At home, I gently give it space in the back of my closet.

Sundays I take Mom to Catholic Mass at the liberal Catholic church—to me, an oxymoron—that Mary Rose has sought out. I haven't been to Mass except at Christmas for nearly three decades, and find my life missing a spiritual community. But as I pray with them, I cannot see a belief system for myself between my mother's literal, and Mary Rose's metaphorical, acceptance of the church's canon. I try for their faith and fail; the spirituality that I feel in nature, and the congregation of our environmental community, will have to be enough for now.

April 8th bodes better weather; Malina can't come and I canvass another Hillsboro neighborhood alone, talking to people and passing out the same flyers. One person is obnoxious, a heavyset gruff man who barks, "I have a construction company. I'm not gonna vote for that. I want to build on all those places." Only later did I think what should have been my response: "The Home Builders Association endorses this ballot measure. The philosophy is that if you save *some* greenspaces, you can build everywhere else and still maintain our quality of life."

Saturday morning, April 22nd, we're sent with a new glossy flyer, paid for by the Nature Conservancy, that says on one side, *"Families. Fun. Forever!"* On the other, it reminds voters, *"Measure 26-26 means more…picnicking, walking, swimming, biking, hiking, bird-watching, jogging, boating and fishing in some of our region's most beautiful open spaces, natural areas, waterways and parks."* We're being directed to neighborhoods that voted a strong "yes" in the previous election. No more knocking on doors and talking to voters; now we're to cover wider areas, leaving flyers in doorways and moving on.

I've picked Laurelhurst, my old neighborhood, and enjoy the unseasonably tropical day, stopping at houses I'd passed on evening strolls for years. Often people who see me coming will open the door, take the flyer in hand and voice ardent support. At one house I climb steep granite stairs past voluptuous gardens. The owner comes out and exclaims, "Of course I support greenspaces. Look at all my flowers. I'd love to help. Have somebody call me and I'll volunteer, too!"

Friday, April 28th, ballots are mailed and a smaller cadre of volunteers heads out during the weekend to stuff eyeball-popping-yellow "Voter Alert" postcards in doorways, reminding people to vote. I've picked a rehabbed neighborhood in the northwest part of the city, and I relish the walking until I realize that many of the streets have new rowhouses that take, I count, 32 steps up and down to leave one card. Even wearing my best walking shoes, the soles of my feet ache. It starts to rain as I shove the last card inside a screen door. I'm glad that the canvassing is over, but I'm not sure of looking forward to the next big, and final, push—phone banks.

Hanging in our hallway is a quote from Liv Ullman that a friend, knowing how much I love it, wrote in calligraphy and framed: "Nothing ever comes to an end. Wherever one has sunk roots that emanate from one's best or truest self, one will always find a home." I take "home" not to mean a physical place, but a place of belonging. Through this campaign, we are all sinking roots of our truest and best selves, and the branches of family reach out and embrace others. Working on the campaign, Dawn and Mary Rose have become friends, and we are all drawn together. Dawn offers to help as I plan a shower for Mary Rose.

"Would you pick up the cake?" I ask first. Then later, inundated with invitations, groceries and cooking, I call back. "Would you *order* the cake, too? I'll pay for it, but will you take care of that whole thing?"

"Of course. I'm delighted to do it. But I'm going to pay for it, so don't argue."

A few days later she elatedly phones back. "I got Barb Macomber's illustration for Ron and Mary Rose's wedding invitation and Three Lions Bakery is going to follow it to decorate the cake." At the shower, we crowd around as Dawn opens the box. No standard wedding bells here. The cake is as splendid as a wildflower meadow, iced with trilliums, Douglas-fir cones, lupine, dogwood and balsamroot blooms.

When everyone else has left, Dawn, Mary Rose and I drive across the island to a bed and breakfast where Mary Rose reserves a room on the beach for the night of the wedding, and, except for Ron knowing, we're sworn to secrecy.

By now, Patricia, Liz and the other funding committee members have raised nearly $300,000. There have been 45 house parties. Sixty thousand dollars were spent hiring people to phone 100,000 households identifying "yes" voters. A hundred thousand pieces of full-color literature have been distributed by volunteers. Audubon donated much of Ron's time to the campaign, and he in turn organized hundreds of volunteers. The staff and volunteers work at headquarters until late each night, including weekends; John Sherman has been there practically every day. Volunteer speakers made presentation to more than a hundred community organizations, throughout all three counties. Nature's Grocery Stores printed 200,000 bags supporting the measure. Five direct mailings went out to tens of thousands of voters. Every day, letters to the editor are published in newspapers around the region, and feature stories appeared on schedule the week the ballots went out. Any time I talk to Liz, or Patricia, or any of the campaign staff, I shower them with praise. We can't possibly lose.

Yet right now Liz is in a panic. John is more upset than I've ever seen him. Extraordinary numbers of ballots are coming in from areas where last time there was a strong "no" vote. And based on past statistics, it's looking like more people will cast ballots than have ever before voted in a mail-in election. If that's true, the 150,001 number on which the whole campaign is based is wrong. Liz takes the chance, even though all the money raised to date has been spent, to hire phone callers in addition to volunteers.

"Phone calls are so easy," the campaign staff has said all along. Anyone who couldn't face going door-to-door was encouraged to sign up for phone banks. In campaign jargon, this climactic stage is called G-O-T-V, Get Out The Vote. We'll spend the next week calling our "yes" voters and reminding them to send in their ballots. After that, we'll buy computer lists showing who has returned their ballots, and call our supporters who haven't. I've signed up for two shifts each week, six to nine in the evenings.

A local business has donated their telemarketing phones to us, and so I sit amid catalog order-takers as I call down my list of 120 names. Immediately I realize I prefer face-to-face canvassing. To me, phone calls in the evening, unless they're from friends, and sometimes even then, are an intrusion. I constantly feel I'm intruding on someone's life, and many who answer let me know with irritation that's true.

Most people have mailed in their ballots, or say they have. So phone banking seems an unpleasant waste of time, except for the 22 people who have forgotten the ballot, and thank me for reminding them. I've learned to think in numbers: 22 votes, times 40 phone-callers is 880 votes per evening, more than 12,000 votes in two weeks that surely would have been lost. It's not fun, but I can see it's worth the effort.

Less than a week before election day, the Trust for Public Land holds a "Yes on 26-26 Party" at a new brewpub, the Portland Brewing Company. The ballots are returning in record numbers, and we have no idea whether that's because we've inspired more people than ever to vote, or whether the "No new taxes" folks are making sure they're heard. Liz pleads for donations to hire more phone callers, and teasingly blames the lack of money on Patricia: "She and Tom Walsh got married last month but she refused to let us use her wedding as a campaign fund-raiser!" TPL has offered to match the evening's contributions, up to five thousand dollars. John Sherman, Mary Rose and others walk through the jovial crowd with beer steins that people stuff with cash and checks.

I take to coming in early for my phone bank volunteering so I can work through my list fast and at least not bother anyone after eight. On my last night, John, who's been phoning every night and even bought his own headset, finishes when I do, but goes back for another list. I can't bear the thought of it. "But Donna," he says, "What if we lose by one vote?" I don't know how to answer him and say nothing. I think to myself, "If we lose by one vote, after all this, I wouldn't believe it had anything to do with me. I did enough." But just the same, I feel guilty as I pick up my purse and leave, hearing John make yet another call.

Unlike general elections, where returns are tallied all day, special mail-in ballots are announced at 8:00 p.m. On May 16th, inside the Oregon Historical Society Center, we follow bright orange optimistic "Victory Party" signs down hallways to an open exhibit area. I've brought my box of more than a thousand pins from the last campaign and set it at the top of the stairs with a sign, "Mementos. Take as many as you'd like." Bob carries two bottles of champagne in a small cooler with ice.

By 7:30 the room is crowded. I'm asked to announce that Liz and the field organizers have gone to the three county offices to pick up the official results and will be there shortly. Just past eight Liz storms up to the microphone and yells, "We won!" We're stunned long enough hear her continue, "Multnomah County, 66 percent YES!" but the shrieking gets too loud and I can barely hear the rest, "Washington County, 59 percent YES! Clackamas County, 58 percent YES!" I whoop and Richard lifts me up and swings me around. Bob and I uncork the champagne and hunt out Liz, Mary Rose, Ron, Patricia and John and we clink glasses in exultant toasts.

The exact figures are released the following day: Yes, 63 percent, 153,204 votes. *The Oregonian* reports, "The margin of victory for Metro's measure was staggering, even to those who worked for it."

This victory really began for me more than two years ago with the Guerrilla Gang for Greenspaces and I want my own celebration to come full circle: I'm going to sleep in the Birdhouse. It was reassembled last autumn on Jeff's 120 acres, back by the seasonal pond, and I've regularly hiked there to see it. Jeff's seven-year-old daughter Lily is the only person enthused about joining me. Devoted Jibo, who will follow me anywhere, is coming too.

The first warm weekend after the election, Bob helps us hoist up the backpacks holding sleeping bags, pads and pillows, and a thermos of hot chocolate and lemon muffins for the morning. I've bought Lily a spiral-bound field journal and waterproof pen like she's seen me use, and she immediately begins to write, "I am in a berd house rite now with my frends dog hows name is jibo..."

We're hardly settled when dusk starts to fall, and we peek out the giant hole as a blue heron hunts for frogs in the pond. After dark, coyotes howl us to sleep. There's a steel mill across the river, and in the middle of the night I awaken and recognize the distant familiar clanging sounds, a world away from Braddock.

Lily giggles as Jibo licks us good morning, the dog's tail swishing like a fan across Lily's hair. She slides farther inside the sleeping bag and Jibo shimmies in after her. *Kill-deer, kill-deer*, a shorebird raucously calls out its name. Lily gives up and we eat breakfast, watching from our silent nest as two wood ducks land in the pond. Through the binoculars, their glossy green, blue, gold and orange feathers glow iridescent in the morning light.

The eve of Mary Rose's wedding, I pick up her Mom at the hotel and together we drive to the airport and wait for Uncle Joe and Aunt Annie, whose name they lovingly run together so that it sounds like AunTannie. A long time ago Mary Rose had asked a special favor: if the women in her family and her other bridesmaids could stay together with her at our house this night. So Bob has been ousted and goes to Jeff's. We women gather here long past the rehearsal and dinner and sit outdoors under falling stars, sharing dreams and daughterly stories.

In the morning I run down to the island farm market for fresh blueberries and peaches and bake them into a cobbler, and grind beans for coffee. Out back on the deck JoJo pins a row of clothespins along the hem of Mary Rose's top, and promises to later tell her their meaning. We think it will be relaxing to walk on the beach, but once we get there euphoria takes hold and we leap-frog and cartwheel along the Columbia's shore. Mary Rose grabs a branch and writes in the sand, "I'm getting married today!"

The wedding is held at Leach Botanical Gardens, with rows of wooden benches and reception tables graced with potted herbs set among sassafras trees, knobcone pines and licorice ferns, native plants and wildflowers. Father Bob Krueger has guided Mary Rose and Ron for months, counseling them for marriage in the Catholic Church and helping them plan their ceremony.

During his sermon, Father Bob says, "I have married only two couples where both the bride and groom were involved in social activism. So in our preparations I have been particularly interested in the spirituality of a married couple related to the concerns of the world around them. Jesus had a deep compassion, which was central to his life and his preaching. He was outward-directed to deal with the issues of justice and peace in the community."

A stream of sunlight falls on the bridal party and the call of a nuthatch punctuates his discourse, and he continues:

"In his letter to the Romans, Paul says, 'Be generous in offering hospitality.' We have two people who lobby and organize for the sake of the environment. It seems to me that hospitality applies there, for what we are attempting to do in our world is to provide a hospitable place for every person." Ron whispers to Mary Rose, just loud enough for some of us to hear, "…and creature."

Audubon's business manager Bob Wilson leads a litany of prayer that Father Bob has written, which includes:

"For those who serve the needs of the human community through their work, their family life and their volunteer efforts, we pray to God." We answer, "Oh God, hear our prayer."

"For a universal appreciation of environment as gift, and a deep sense of our relationship to it, with an understanding of our responsibility for its health, we pray to God."

"God, hear our prayer."

As part of the ceremony's ending, Father Bob adds, "And may they reach old age in the company of their friends."

At twilight, Mary Rose and Ron grab tapers from the candelabra and lead a Conga line. I catch up with her and we dance, earth sisters, shoes kicked aside, stocking feet twirling in the grass, amid the fairy bells, amid the snow queens, amid the fawn lilies, amid the lady ferns, amid the shooting stars, as the twangy notes of the steel drum harmonize with the nuthatch's last song of dusk.

Chapter 17
This Land Across Time

Hailstones the size of marbles beat against my gloved hands as I tamp pungent earth around a red osier dogwood. Fred Nachtigal, a few plant holes away, looks cold in his thin denim jacket and jeans. Bryce Jacobson, Tim Braun and Jerome DeGraaff round out the Conservancy's group, joining three Multnomah County Parks employees in the restoration of the Bybee Howell Territorial Park wetland.

Beneath unexpected scudding slate clouds we had gathered early this morning, April 4th, 1992. Over 140 trees and shrubs await our work, bundles of thin stalks with filigreed roots in five-gallon buckets. Dirt-caked shovels lay strewn against the fence until everyone arrived. County landscapers had come earlier in the week to loosen the sod, or our task would be much harder.

We headed off in groups of two, matching Pete Schiedeman's restoration plant to the holes—a thimbleberry here, big leaf maple there. One person spreads the roots then holds the slim stick of a plant in position. The other crumbles the soil, hand-pulverizing the clods into loose dirt, gently layering it over the roots. When the stalk is in place, we shove a wooden stake next to it and finish by stomping the dirt to compress any air pockets out from around the roots. The bucket brigade follows, pouring water over the new plant, stomping, pouring, stomping. On to the next. Pete says these plants are native species, but not necessarily genetic to Sauvie Island.

What of native? There's no chance to restore the native species of *homo sapiens,* though it's not hard, down in the marsh, in a spot where houses and barns aren't visible, to imagine life in this wet land 200 years ago. If I were a 43-year-old woman here then, I would be a Chinook Indian, Multnomah tribe. Winter or summer I'd be barefoot, bare-legged, clothed with a mantle of animal skins and a fringed skirt of cedar bark that reached to my thighs. My long black hair, parted down the middle, uncombed, would be anointed with fish oil, my face painted red. I'd wear ornaments of white shells called *hiaqua,* Indian money. And I'd be a flathead. I'd have done to my children what my parents did to me: tie the baby to a flat board, then fix another piece of wood across the brow, pressuring the skull to flatten in a continuous line from crown to nose. If this didn't prove fatal, the child would grow to life marked with superiority and distinction.

In April, 1792, 200 years before today, no white person would have yet stepped foot on the island. White exploration of the Columbia River began the following month when Captain Robert Gray traveled 36 miles upriver, still 50-odd miles short of here. Six months later a naval expedition led by Captain George Vancouver aimed to venture farther. Vancouver sent Lieutenant William Broughton to survey the Columbia for the British Admiralty, and he reached this island. My father, husband and sons might have been among the 150 warriors who arrived in 23 canoes to see the paleface when he landed on the rocks at the island's northern end. Indians from another river tribe who accompanied Broughton explained his mission, and the islanders welcomed the men and stayed to trade. That night, the British explorers slept here. Broughton named the location Point Warrior. Today's name of Warrior Rock still bears the remembrance of the occasion.

The hailstorm subsides and the sun pries its beams through a sky-field of clouds. We stop to share a thermos of coffee, the warmth encouraging to our chilled bodies. The trees and shrubs we're planting snake along the outskirts of the rushes that encircle the pond's open water. First are Pacific willows, *salix lasiandra,* seven shiny reddish twigs that as trees eventually branch out into a thicket, 20 to 50 feet high. Next, ten red alder, *alnus rubra*. They grow to 100 feet, graceful trees with a mottled nearly-white bark. The winged nutlets they produce helicopter to the ground, spreading seeds across a broad expanse. Nestled between the stands of trees are two *rosa rugosa,* fragrant wild roses bearing large orange hips, high in Vitamin C, that birds devour. Another nine Pacific willow, then ten thimbleberry, *rubus parviflorus.* The thimble-shaped red fruit of these brambling shrubs are as well a feast for dozens of birds and animals.

Across the pond I can see a small patch of wapato, *sagittaria latifolia,* named after the constellation Sagittarius, the centaur shooting an arrow. A worldly plant also known as arrowhead or wild potato, it's been highly cultivated by the Chinese. I recognized its leaves on a swamp tour in Louisiana. County Parks' staff is encouraging the regeneration of wapato, once a staple of the native islanders' diet.

As a Multnomah tribeswoman 200 years ago, harvesting wapato would have been one of my major responsibilities. I would have a canoe of my own, about 12 feet long, 20 inches wide, 9 inches deep. I'd carry it to the edge of a pond, then take off my clothes, put them in the boat and float it alongside as I wade to the wapato. The water might come to my armpits as I feel in the mud with my feet, digging in, following the roots with my toes until I reach a bulb. Loosened, it would float to the surface. I might spend several hours collecting enough wapato to fill the canoe. Enough for my family to roast fresh on embers, to dry and store, and to trade with other tribes.

This piece of wet land adjoining high ground might well have been the site of one of the island's 15 Multnomah villages. I would have been amongst the 2,000 islanders living here in cedar log houses 30 yards long and a dozen yards wide. Our family, like each of the others, would have its own entrance and fire pit within. Just beyond the marsh, in the meadow, is a centuries-old oak. Its acorns would have been the source for our favorite delicacy—Chinook olives. The men would pile the acorns into a basket set in a hole outside the entrance, covered with grass and then dirt. For four to five months, all of us in the family would urinate on that spot, after which time we'd remove the treats and enjoy them with gusto.

We plant five Douglas spirea, *spiraea douglasii,* rounding the first bend. These shrubs are topped with pink pyramid-shaped flower clusters on branches with such tough, wiry stems that the plant is also known as hardhack. At the point of the bend goes a bigleaf maple, *acer macrophyllum.* Its leaves can grow as long as ten inches, turning brilliant orange-red before they drop in autumn. Natives used the wood to make canoe paddles. Squirrels and bees, woodpeckers and sapsuckers, song sparrows and other birds all enjoy the maple's bounty.

Along the next length more spirea, willow and roses are connected to a dozen red osier dogwood and five Oregon ash. The dogwood, *cornus stolonifera*, is named after the Old English *dagge*, or dagger, for the wood is so hard it was used in Europe to make butcher skewers. "Osier" is a name given to willows whose pliable twigs are often used for baskets and furniture. These stalks are deep red and grow to ten feet tall, producing clusters of white-petaled flowers which become small white fruit. The adjoining Oregon ash, *fraxinus latifolia,* could grow to 80 feet. There is a superstition in the northwest that wherever this tree grows, there are no poisonous snakes, which is true here.

The island's rich alluvial soil should nurture these infant trees and shrubs. From the Pleistocene Era a million years ago, earth from the mountains upriver on the Columbia washed down with the rains and snowmelt, swirling in eddies, thrashing over waterfalls, to come to a stop at a ledge of large rocks that form the island's north end. Through those eons, soil accumulated in minute increments to a depth of 30 feet, in some places 50, topsoil a rich one-inch icing. Each year the inundation continued, with annual freshets layering mud and sand, eventually shaping the earth into soft rolling contours, peppered with dozens of lakes and ponds. The island is a river-bottom landscape unique in the West.

Lewis and Clark literally put the place on the map during their explorations of 1805 and 1806, when they named it Wappato Island. It was populated by 2,000 natives, who during the next decades weathered outbreaks of smallpox, syphilis, measles and tuberculosis. Then in 1829 a horrifying epidemic of a fever known as the *ague* swept across the land. Within two years, the natives were nearly extinct. If I had been a fortunate woman at the time, my own convulsive agony would have come early, before I had to watch the excruciating death of everyone I loved. Those with strength remaining would have wrapped my body in mats and placed it in my canoe, and left my bones to rest there in the branches of a tall tree.

The white-skinned people brought disease and death that changed the human-scape of the island. What they brought next—cattle—changed the landscape, and led to today's restoration. Less than a decade after the island became uninhabited by humans, the Hudson Bay Company, with its Fort Vancouver just across the Columbia, sent a French dairyman, Laurent Sauvé, to establish a dairy near the site of this wetland. Around 400 cattle were swum across the river from the fort. Sauvé was to produce butter for the Russian settlements in Alaska with whom Hudson Bay had a contract. The island came to take his name.

Not long after Sauvé began the dairy, in 1845, a party from the Savannah Oregon Immigration Society set out from Missouri across the Oregon Trail. Four of the 64 wagons carried Robert E. Miller, his wife Sara Fergueson, eight of their 11 children, and their families. They arrived on Sauvé's island and settled near each other. The land where we plant today was claimed by the Millers' daughter Julia Ann and her husband, James Francis Bybee.

In 1850 the U.S. Congress passed the Donation Land Act to reward pioneers for their hardships in settling the West. A married couple could claim 640 acres, half for the husband, half for the wife. Until the land was all taken, girls 11 and 12 were married to older men who could then double their claims. The girls lived at home with their parents until they were old enough to be proper brides. My land down the road is named for the island's first claimants, Jacob and Mary Cline, pioneers from Illinois. The deed reads, "Beginning at the most westerly corner of the Jacob Cline Donation Land Claim, thence..." James F. and Julia Bybee were the third claimants. Both Jacob Cline and James Bybee arrived on Sauvé's land impoverished and headed, as did many pioneers, down to the great California gold rush. Both found gold, and Bybee returned with enough money to build the nine-room classical Greek Revival house that stands restored on the property today.

From the time of Sauvé and the Bybees, who in 1873 sold the property to John and Joseph Howell, this land was grazed by cattle.

John Howell and his bride Amelia moved into the house and raised four children here.

One of their descendants, Marjorie Tabor, now lives on adjoining property called Arrowhead Acres. She wrote a letter of support for this project, stating, "I have long been a guardian of wildlife on Howell Park. The potential for people enjoying the park without harm to the environment is great on this special piece of land. I will do all I can to help you." Multnomah County bought the Bybee Howell property in 1960 and restored the house, now listed on the National Register of Historic Places, to its 1855-1885 vintage. The 93-acre Howell Territorial Park includes the house, wetlands, agricultural museum, pioneer orchard, pasture and picnic grounds. Marge's cows have been permitted to graze on the land and she, in turn, has pumped water from Dairy Creek into the pond at her own expense when it dries up each summer. The dearth of water is a legacy of the dikes built in the 1940s to prevent the annual freshets.

Over the years, the traditional pasturing of the cows destroyed the wetland pond banks. As the cattle moved to drink from the water, their hooves eroded the banks and damaged riparian vegetation. Their presence also limited the variety of wetland and upland plants that could survive. Besides the planting, the restoration includes fencing off the cattle and installing a pump to provide water for vegetation and wildlife year-round. It was one of 14 projects awarded a Demonstration Grant from the Metropolitan Greenspaces program, funded by the U.S. Department of Fish and Wildlife. Multnomah County matched the $10,000 grant with another $10,000. The grant proposal listed my name as one of eight under "Project Staff and Volunteers."

More red osiers, thimbleberry and red alder round another curve. Then a stretch of berries—salmonberry, thimbleberry, and serviceberry. Salmonberry, *rubus spectabilis,* is a spectacle with its remarkable salmon-colored fruit. The natives ate the plants' shoots as well as its berries, which birds and animals find a feast. The Western serviceberry, *amelanchier alnifolia,* is more tree than berry bush at 30 feet high. Its dark purple fruits are like small apples, popular with the flicker, thrush and scarlet tanager. More thimbleberries, another big leaf maple, then six plants of elderberries, *sambucus canadensis*. Rose-breasted grosbeaks, jays and a variety of songbirds love the berries of this plant, named for the Greek *sambuse,* an ancient musical instrument. More thimbleberries, then five black cottonwood trees, *populus trichocarpa*, whose soft downy seeds spread like clouds of cotton across the upland. These are the tallest of today's planting, and could grow to 120 feet.

Now the sun has disappeared behind a swath of menacing clouds and a hard rain begins. Just past noon, the temperature is dropping swiftly. I shiver with each cool breeze that whips across and through my already-soaked clothing. Then a second, ferocious, hailstorm thunders, pelting biting balls of ice against our exposed skin. Fred's hands are raw. My face burns. Dan Kromer, the county's project manager, gathers us together and we agree to leave, 20 plants short of finishing. A staff person from the county will come next week to put in the remaining upland salmonberry, thimbleberry and cottonwoods.

Wintering-In is held the last Saturday each September at Howell Territorial Park. The Historical Society invites everyone to usher in autumn with bluegrass music, a barbecue, old photo and book sale and craft fair. I always head first to the table offering free cider pressed fresh from the old Gravenstein, Cranberry Pippin, Roxbury Russett and hundred other varieties of apples from the Pioneer Orchard. Last year during Wintering-In I lead two Wetlands Walks to the marsh. At 12:30 and 2:30 the hikes were announced over the loudspeaker, and each time about a dozen people, from four years old to 74, came along. I asked two children to carry the high-powered spotting scopes I'd borrowed from Mike Houck. From the edge of a hill overlooking the pond we got a close look at pintails, mallards, cinnamon teal and great blue heron. A nutria peered out from the rushes and scrambled back in surprise. Redwing blackbirds whistled their flirty song, a bald eagle soared overhead, a red-tailed hawk swooped by and landed on a branch of an oak.

The last group dispersed and I walked back to the House for Autumn, a temporary, contemporary work of art called a site-sculpture by the artist, Helen Lessick. From the outside, it looked like a storybook house, made of three tons of Sauvie Island straw, fescue actually, grown on the island for cattle feed and bedding. Helen had built the structure using baled straw like large rough-hewn bricks, then thatched a roof with local grasses. I'd been in the house before, but wanted to come back. Inside, the playhouse aura ended and I felt softly enveloped by the earth, the scent of hay all-encompassing, a soft golden light muted through the walls and ceiling. At the far end, two bales provided an enticing seat, a place of simple meditation on the straw and the land. The previous Sunday had been the autumnal equinox, and Helen had created a performance at the House with storytellers and Native Americans drumming up the Sun Dance. The House was intended to decay over time, its natural deterioration part of its art and purpose. Helen took it down the first day of winter, returning the decaying plant material to the site. In its own way, it was, for a time, a native presence on the island.

What of native? What is to be the natural, or unnatural succession of this place? My grandmothers both lived around four score. I wonder if I shall walk here someday, a wrinkled lady with a cane, and look past lush vegetation up 120 feet to watch a rough-legged hawk land in a cottonwood I once planted. My bones belong here, too. We are all part of the island's story, all part of this land across time.

Epilogue

A revival meeting, that's what it's like! A thigh-slapping, arms-flailing, spirit-rocking revival meeting! Gospel of the Evangelical Environmentalists. It's April 23, 2008, and a 20-year celebration of Metropolitan Greenspaces at—where else—the Bridgeport Brewpub (and now Bakery).

I'm up first with the opening scenes of a film that Odyssey produced and I wrote, commissioned to tell the story about the greenspaces program once it was up and running. The narration begins, "In the mellow gold of dawn, wings stretch and soar, over a landscape where a vision has been launched—to protect places of nature, spaces yet green, nurturing the lives of all who abide there. And so around the city, it's still possible to discover (tah-dah, the title) The Nature of Metropolitan Greenspaces."

I tell the crowd that this is the smooth, after-the-fact, seem-so-easy story, and introduce Mike Houck, who will present the behind the scenes saga of the rough and tumble, down and dirty, chomp-your-fingernails, long, long, exciting and challenging adventure that brought us here to Greenspaces.

Looking around those gathered, I think about how all our lives have changed since I began keeping journals of our stories. Mary Rose Navarro and Ron Carley have a son and daughter, Nicolas and Elena, for whom nature is an intrinsic part of life. Ron is now co-director of

Coalition for a Livable Future and Mary Rose works for Metro Parks and Greenspaces. Ali Highberger and Dan Weig are married, too, with a son Nick who loves the outdoors.

My mom has passed away; also Jim Charlton, Bob Murase, Larry Kressel, Fred Nachtigal, Marge Tabor, Uncle George, Nissa and Jibo. I joined the Unitarian Universalist church, drawn by its calling of world-healing activism and spirituality. Bob Stephens and I are divorced now nearly ten years. Lily Joslin and Bob's niece Chynna Stephens shared in many of my camping, hiking, kayaking and other outdoors adventures. For the past six years I've been enjoying life with my partner Steve Bleiler and his daughter Aly, who have joined in many conservation efforts.

In November, 1994 I was honored by KGW-TV and Portland General Electric with a citizenship award as a "Citizen Who Cares" and featured in a 30-second public service announcement that ran in prime time throughout the month.

Willamette Week newspaper's annual "Best of Portland" issue in 1995 included me and the Sauvie Island Conservancy as "Best Island Defenders." The award citation begins, "Imaging driving to Sauvie Island and seeing a swank new golf course. A lot of people thought it was a lousy idea. Some people actually did something about it."

Issues small and large have never stopped. Another greenspaces bond measure, this time for $227.4 million, went on the ballot in November, 2006. Instead of purchasing 6,000 acres with the 1995 measure, Metro was able to parlay the dollars into the acquisition of 8,100 acres of significant natural areas. That success led voters to lean favorably toward Measure 26-80. Liz Kaufman lead the campaign, which won with a resounding 64 percent victory. Despite passing them out repeatedly as mementos, I still have more than 1,000 campaign buttons from the first bond measure in my office.

The biggest disaster the island faced was Measure 37, a 2004 bond measure that undermined Oregon's land use laws. It was advertised as a way for property owners to build a few houses on their land if that was allowed when they bought their property, irregardless of current land use laws. More than 7,500 claims were filed, including massive developments on farm and forestlands.

On Sauvie Island, Measure 37 claims covered more than 750

acres of farmland, requesting subdivisions and significant waterfront development along Multnomah Channel. Within a few weeks of the filing deadline, we had an email working group of 45 people, and held an island-wide public meeting to alert neighbors. We helped campaign to the state legislature to put Measure 49 on the ballot, which would limit the right to build subdivisions and large developments. Liz Kaufman led that campaign, too. Jeanne Bevis, Mary Forst and I organized a splendid evening garden party fundraiser at Sean Hogan's renowned Cistus Nursery on the island, and raised more than $5,000. Election night, we were euphoric at the victory party—Measure 49 passed handily, with a 68 percent yes vote.

Mike Houck won a Lowe Fellowship at Harvard and took a year's sabbatical. I was hired part-time by Audubon to handle some of the public outreach part of his work and helped lead a "Ribbons of Green" campaign to protect natural resources throughout the region. Mike remains Audubon's Urban Naturalist and is founder and director of the Urban Greenspaces Institute. Jim Labbe, in taking over Ron's old job as Audubon Urban Conservationist, expanded FAUNA's activism.

Dave Fouts retired as a respiratory therapist and still devotes time to his purple martin houses. The Oregon Department of Fish and Wildlife now has an Oregon Conservation Strategy that includes better protection for species like purple martins. Jeff Joslin is senior design review planner for the City of Portland. Lily Joslin is in college, embarking on a program of environmental studies. Marcia Hoyt owns the Historic Lantz House Inn bed and breakfast in Centerville, Indiana, which boasts five award-winning native plant gardens. Jesse, Malina and Sky McKenzie are grown and continue to relish adventures in the outdoors.

Multnomah County Parks were transferred to Metro Parks and Greenspaces. Virginia Lakes now goes by the official name of Wapato Access Greenway State Park. A few hummingbirds have stayed through the winter at my place for the past two years. Howard Blumenthal is still paddling. Beverly Stein ran for governor in the Democratic primary in 2002; after losing she became a co-owner of the Public Strategies Group, which works to transform governments nationwide.

The word "grassroots" seems an apt term for us. I have cleared grass roots from many places on my property, for vegetables, flowers, ecolawn. Grass roots grow deep and strong. They are tenacious and tough to get rid of. They spread heartily.

Tonight isn't just a celebration of Metropolitan Greenspaces, it's the launch of Connecting Green Alliance, a program that aims for no less than "creating the world's greatest system of parks, trails and natural areas." Government agencies, nonprofits, private companies and individuals are invited to collectively transcend turf and state boundaries to protect more of our unique natural inheritance.

At the end of the evening, a large poster is propped on an easel. It's blank except for the Connecting Green Alliance logo. We are all invited to join in the Alliance. From around the room, people line up from Oregon and Washington to announce their names in the microphone and sign up on the poster. Each name followed by whoops and applause.

"I'm Meryl Redisch for Portland Audubon."

"Glenn Lamb with the Columbia Land Trust."

"Dave Beckett with Three Rivers Land Conservancy"

"Kelly Puteney, Clark County"

And near the end of the line, me, "Sauvie Island Conservancy." The poster is so full there's barely room to squeeze in our name.

A revival? The word no longer seems an appropriate description. This collection of grassroots environmentalists has never dissipated enough to need reviving. It's a reunion. Earth sisters and earth brothers. An earth family reunion.

Appendix

Becoming a Grassroots Environmentalist

Each of us must do our part,
no matter where we live, in city or
countryside, in Africa, America
or elsewhere. When people care,
one by one, they multiply this hope
again and again, and only then is there change.

Jane Goodall

If you would like to contribute in some measure to protecting our environment, whether it's two hours a month or ten dollars on occasion, the following Appendix will help you begin. It includes information about organizations that would appreciate any help you might volunteer, and advice on how to start your own conservation efforts for your favorite place.

How to Get Involved

This advice is drawn from three workshops that I organized when leading FAUNA, to help conservation activists become more effective. "The Basics of Public Speaking" was developed by Beverly Stein, then an Oregon state representative; and Alison Highberger, then co-producer of KATU-TV's weekly "Town Hall" show. "How to Start a Friends Group" was a panel that included Jeffry Gottfried, co-founder, Fans of Fanno Creek; Althea Broome, co-founder, the Wetlands Conservancy; Kathleen Maloney, community organizer who worked for 1000 Friend of Oregon; and Richard Seidman, founder of Friends of Trees. "How to Promote Your Group's Events" was created by Marcia Hoyt, then advertising manager for Portland General Electric.

Find Some Friends

The first step in getting involved as a grassroots environmentalist is finding some like-minded people with whom you can share a commitment. If you don't have a pressing agenda of your own, offer to volunteer for a local wildlife or environmental group. Chapters of national organizations like Audubon, the Nature Conservancy, the Sierra Club and others are always looking for help. Often state fish and wildlife departments and state, county and city parks have active volunteer groups. Maybe you've gone to some conservation event you've enjoyed—like the Salmon Festival or Wild Arts Festival—where your energy would be appreciated. Whether you have special skills like graphic design or computer programming, or enjoy simple tasks like answering the phone or stuffing envelopes, your contribution will be an enormous benefit.

What if you *do* have a hot issue—a manufacturing plant is dumping sewage in a creek, you'd love to see a trail built along an unused railway, a developer wants to chop down a stately old oak. Begin by seeking out some collaborators. It's possible to tackle a campaign on your own, but it's time-consuming, expensive, and can be wearying. To find others, look for people who are directly affected by the issue. They might be neighbors, co-workers or others in the community who would value what you propose.

Organizing pros will tell you that the best way to inspire people to join your conservation efforts is to simply ask—and to ask in person. Face-to-face discussion gives an issue a feeling of importance and it gives you the chance to get better acquainted with the potential volunteer regarding the subject. And when you do ask, be enthusiastic. Don't apologize or belittle the nature of what you want to see accomplished.

You might be amazed at the support you garner. In Portland, people who were appalled at the imminent destruction of the "Corbett Street Oak" organized Friends of the Oak and drew together 300 members. They saved the tree.

Of course, you're not likely to gather 300 people in a hurry by asking in person. Other community organizing techniques include inviting people to coffees and potlucks, posting notices in appropriate locations, sending flyers to people who are interested, and networking through the internet.

Get Official

No matter if you're a group of five, you can look impressive on paper, and well you should. Letterhead will speak for you throughout hallowed offices and marbled hallways. You need a name and a logo that epitomize your mission. The Sauvie Island Conservancy's logo is a simple pen and ink illustration of two pintails in reeds, our name, and the subtitle, "dedicated to the preservation of rural life, wildlife and natural recreation areas." This letterhead's total cost was $16.95—the $9.95 source of the drawing, *Animals: 1419 Copyright-free Illustrations of Mammals, Birds, Fish and Insects* (Dover Publications, 1979) and $7 to take the graphic designer to lunch, who volunteered to select type faces and paste up a layout, which we photocopy for our stationery and newsletters.

Behind the scenes, your group can be as formal or informal as you like. If you want to become a non-profit organization, you'll need to file for a 501c3 designation, which includes writing bylaws and forming an official Board of Directors. The non-profit designation, however, severely limits political activism.

Decide on an address or rent a post office box, establish dues, open a bank account, create a membership list, and perhaps initiate a newsletter. Elect officers or designate a key contact person. With most small groups, that person's phone number is the one used for the organization. Determine when and where you'll hold meetings.

Weave a Network

Make connection with existing organizations, especially large conservation groups. When you're trying to get the attention of public officials, it helps to have an accumulation of letters from prominent organizations representing their membership supporting your issue. Suddenly you have thousands of people behind your cause.

Do Your Homework

Credibility will be the cornerstone of your organization. If you're to be at all successful, those you approach to make decisions must be able to trust the information you present. You have to be honest. You have to know not only your stuff, but the other guy's stuff as well.

Beverly Stein says it's integral to become well-versed in the three Ps—Policy, Politics and Personalities. Research the policies behind your subject matter. Intimately understand the history and context of the issue. Be aware of your opponent's arguments. General comments such as "I don't like..." won't hold much sway. You have to be able to focus on the problems in terms of public policy and relevant laws.

Every issue is enmeshed in a political realm. Maybe the governor who supports your cause announces he won't run for re-election and his lame duck status adversely affects your situation. Or there's suddenly public outrage at a polluter's fouling the river and you might coast to victory on the voters' sentiments. Politics and political timing matter immensely. It's important to know your issue's place in the larger picture.

Then you have to consider the politicians themselves. They know who are their supporters. They are human, and while they make decisions based on their integrity, you can work to influence them. Develop a relationship with your elected officials so they trust you. Work on the campaigns of people you'd like to see get elected. Try to find a champion from inside. Check voting records. Is a particular politician vulnerable right now and needs the support of your block of constituents? Part of your research is finding the right buttons to push with each elected official whose vote you need.

Get Political

Before long, you'll find yourself speaking at a public hearing. If you've done your homework, you have lots of significant things to say. Now you need to focus on how to present your views most effectively.

Don't try to say everything yourself. Organize a lineup of speakers, and make sure many of them are experts in their fields—wildlife biologists, wetlands experts and so forth. Their testimony will carry a lot of weight. It's also very effective to include young people. Determine the time limit the hearing allots for each speaker—often only three minutes, with a buzzer that requires you to finish that sentence then stop talking. Discuss with everyone what aspect of the issue they'll address and have them write out and time with a stopwatch what they expect to say. You don't want to be cut off before you get to the main point you want to make.

To arrange the order of speakers, follow the basic elements of producing a performance: Begin with something that will grab the audience's attention. Then move into a rhythm and flow—perhaps soft-spoken speakers alternated with more energetic and boisterous ones. And give great consideration to who will go last—what thought you want to leave people with. It's often a good idea to save some people (and allotted minutes) for the end to rebut any convincing arguments that arise from the opposition during the hearing.

Dress up. Look your public best. It gives you credibility. Even though you've prepared what you want to say, when you testify, don't read it. Know it well, look directly at the officials, and talk. As Beverly Stein says, "Speak from the heart. There's nothing more appealing."

Be positive and upbeat. Give your qualifications and get to the point. Don't take longer than the allotted time. If somebody before you said essentially what you planned to say, don't repeat it. Just add that you support so-and-so's comments. Ask specifically for what you want. Don't attack, and don't burn your bridges. Sometimes you'll lose; don't lash out. Visual aids—maps, slides and videos—can be extremely effective at carrying your message with immediacy. Consider the politicians or officials who have been sitting there for hours. As one commented, "We like to be entertained." Well-researched and powerfully presented face-to-face testimony can be as dramatic as a television mystery and is often more potent at changing minds than hundreds of letters and petitions.

Be thoughtful of your language. Give names to places and remarkable flora and fauna you want to save. Don't say "the drainage ditch." Call it "the tributary of Balch Creek, the source of clean water for…" In all the county reports of the Tualatin mountains they were referred to as "the west hills." I refused to call them hills; "mountains" evokes a stronger emotional response. Language has a symbolism and the words you choose are important.

If you're fighting a well-funded opponent with an attorney, make sure you bring your own "grey suit"—either a *pro bono* attorney who will volunteer to help at no charge, or drum up the money to pay an attorney's fees for a bit of prep work and showing up at the hearing. We defeated a proposal where we estimate the developer spent about a quarter-million dollars, and we spent $1,200 on an attorney. Despite your best planning and research, a hearing, just like a trial, can bring forth all sorts of unexpected twists. More times than I can recall, while we were sputtering at some bewildering or outrageous turn of events, our attorney recognized what was going on, knew the legal path through the quandary and ad-libbed brilliantly to save the day.

Become Media-Savvy

Television, radio, newspapers and the internet can carry your message to a vast audience and can have enormous impact on the political climate. Create a media list and plan a communications campaign.

To get television coverage, you need an event that's visual;

remember that you're selling pictures. Make it newsworthy, give it a twist. Consciously plan the timing—Saturdays and Sundays are slow news days, and more likely to be covered, but will generate a smaller audience. News broadcasts are typically at noon, 5:00 and 11:00, so you have to allow time for a producer to shoot the event, get back to the station and edit a story in time to get it on the air.

Two weeks in advance, send a succinct, well-written, one-page press release. At the TV station where Alison Highberger worked, about one story out of 100 press releases actually gets covered, so you need to make yours as appealing as possible. Send a Media Advisory version of the release a week before the event, and prepare a Fact Sheet to hand out to media people who attend. Then phone the station the day before the event, and again early that morning, between 7:00 and 8:30 a.m.

Spend time in advance prepping people to speak on camera. Learn sound bites; think of crisp, perhaps clever one-line quotes that encapsulate your message. It's good if they're ten seconds or less; avoid being a "motor mouth." Consider what questions you might be asked and plan for answers. Don't wear distracting things, like a big hat. If you feel you've bungled a response, ask if you can try again. Reporters want you to look good. You might find yourself an "expert" they'll call on when similar issues arise.

For radio, follow essentially the same format. The press release you send to a newspaper should include a photograph. Some smaller papers will print your photo and story as written. You also can generate a Letters to the Editor campaign. And many newspapers give space to readers' editorials or In My Opinion columns that are excellent forums for airing your perspective to a large audience.

The internet offers seemingly endless possibilities for getting out a message, including YouTube videos, electronic newsletters and websites covering your issue.

Find More Friends

With any group, burnout is inevitable. Even the most ardent conservationists may drop out for awhile, or have less time to contribute. You'll need to continually renew your supply of volunteers. Sometimes people will hear about you, be inspired by what you're doing and seek you out. Other times you'll have to try and actively encourage people to join. Look for every opportunity to do that—many Earth Day and other environmental events offer the chance to set up a table and recruit volunteers. Prepare a brochure about your group and arrange a photo display to attract people to your agenda.

Develop Pro-Active Projects

It's not healthy for your own psyche, or your group's image, to feel that you're always "against" something, or trying to stop something. Be sure to include projects that are nurturing: Restore a wetland. Start a land trust, and actually purchase natural areas. Reach out and spread the work to others, speaking at schools, taking students and teachers on field trips, writing educational material. Offer greenspace tours through your city's bureau of parks. Help create wildlife refuges. Work to improve habitat policy. Volunteer for bird counts and field studies. Help with political campaigns of candidates and issues important to you. Besides feeling wonderful and immeasurably spreading your conservation knowledge and values, you'll build goodwill and help create a positive image for your organization.

Remember to Celebrate!

"Who's bringing the champagne?" is one of the Sauvie Island Conservancy's favorite lines. It's important to have fun and celebrate. Mark each victory with a special event—Sunday brunch on a riverhouse, a picnic paddle, a champagne dinner. Even celebrate a loss, because through your efforts, the public must have learned something that will be of value later.

Laugh a lot. Thank each other. Congratulate each other. Let yourselves feel exultant, feel proud, feel delighted that you have truly helped save the world, if just a small part of it. "Think globally, act locally" is environmentalism's motto. You're doing just that. Go often to the place you've protected, and appreciate your work. Thank reporters and public officials. Heap praise on those who have helped.

Look for formal and meaningful ways to recognize people. Last autumn, on a hike through an ancient forest during the Salmon Festival, I was stopped by a plaque set in stone that named these woods "The Pauline Anderson Forest." More than anyone, Pauline had protected our county's natural resources as a county commissioner. One of her most memorable legacies was a fund that allots money from the sale of county property to purchase natural areas. She's retired now, but still vibrant, and alive to see a magnificent forest bear her name. Everyone who passes through there can be inspired by her work.

The earth needs heroes and heroines. When you contribute your time, energy and money to conservation work, recognize that you are one of them. Enjoy, and celebrate!

Conservation Organizations
Personal Favorites

National

American Rivers
Dedicated to the protection and restoration of North America's rivers
1101 14th Street NW
Suite 1400
Washington, DC 20005
Phone: (202) 347-7550
Fax: (202) 347-9240
www.americanrivers.org

Bat Conservation International
Bat education, conservation and scientific research
P.O. Box 162603
Austin, TX 78716
Phone: (512) 327-9721
Fax: (512) 327-9724
www.batcon.org

Defenders of Wildlife
Saving imperiled wildlife and championing the Endangered Species Act
1130 17th Street, NW
Washington, DC 20036
1-800-385-9712 (toll-free 24/7)
www.defenders. org

Earth First!
Front-line, direct action approach to protecting wilderness
www.earthfirst.org

Earth Island Institute
Conservation, preservation, and restoration of the global environment
300 Broadway, Suite 28
San Francisco, CA 94133-3312
Phone: (415) 788-3666
Fax: (415) 788-7324
www.earthisland.org

Greenpeace
Actively working to address threats to the planet
702 H Street, NW
Washington, D.C. 20001
(202) 462-1177
www.greenpeace.org

Lighthawk
Volunteer-based environmental aviation organization offering aerial perspectives for critical issues
PO Box 653
Lander, WY 82520
Phone: (307) 332-3242
Fax: (888) 297-0156
www.lighthawk.org

National Audubon Society
Conservation and restoration of natural ecosystems, focusing on birds and other wildlife
225 Varick Street, 7th floor
NY, NY 10014
(212) 979-3000
www.audubon.org

National Wildlife Federation
Inspiring people to protect wildlife for our children's future
11100 Wildlife Center Drive
Reston, VA 20190-5362
1-800-822-9919
www.nwf.org

The Nature Conservancy
Purchases land around the world for habitat protection
4245 North Fairfax Drive, Suite 100
Arlington, VA 22203-1606
(703) 841-5300
www.nature.org

Sierra Club
America's oldest and largest grassroots environmental organization
85 Second Street, 2nd Floor
San Francisco, CA 94105
Phone: (415) 977-5500
Fax: (415) 977-5799
www.sierraclub.org

The Trust for Public Land
Help with land conservation projects and ballot measures
116 New Montgomery St., 4th Floor
San Francisco, CA 94105
Phone: (415) 495-4014
FAX (415) 495-4103
1-800-714-LAND
www.tpl.org

World Wildlife Fund
The largest multinational conservation organization in the world
1250 Twenty-Fourth Street, N.W.
Washington, DC 20090-7180
(202) 293-4800
www.worldwildlife.org

Portland Oregon and Region

Audubon Society of Portland
Promoting enjoyment, understanding and protection of native birds and other wildlife and their habitats
5151 NW Cornell Rd.
Portland, OR 97210
Phone: (503) 292-6855
FAX (503) 292-1021
www.audubonportland.org

Columbia Land Trust
Preservation of lands along the Columbia River, Pacific Coast and estuary, Columbia Gorge and eastern Cascade watersheds
1351 Officers' Row
Vancouver, Washington 98661
Phone: (360) 696-0131
FAX: (360) 696-1847
www.columbialandtrust.org

1000 Friends of Oregon
Education and advocacy as the citizens' voice for sound land use planning
534 SW Third Ave., Suite 300
Portland, OR 97204
(503) 497-1000
www.friends.org

Riverkeepers: Columbia Riverkeeper
Restoring and protecting the water quality of the entire Columbia River and all life connected to it
724 Oak Street
Hood River, OR 97031
Phone: (541) 387-3030
Fax (541) 387-3029
www.columbiariverkeeper.org

Riverkeepers: Tualatin Riverkeepers
Working to protect and restore the Tualatin River system
12360 SW Main Street, Suite 100
Tigard, OR 97233
Phone: (503) 620-7505
FAX: (503) 620-7645
www.tualatinriverkeepers.org

Riverkeepers: Willamette Riverkeeper
Working to enable the Willamette to function more naturally, with cold, clean water, and provide healthy habitat for fish and wildlife
Portland Boathouse:
1515 SE Water Ave #102
Portland, Oregon 97214
Phone: (503) 223-6418
Fax: (503) 228-1960
www.willamette-riverkeeper.org

Three Rivers Land Conservancy
Conservation of private natural land in the watersheds of the Clackamas, Tualatin, and lower Willamette Rivers
PO Box 1116
Lake Oswego, Oregon 97035
Phone: (503) 699-9825
Fax: (503) 699-9827
www.trlc.org

For more information about these and hundreds of other national, regional and local conservation organizations check the *Encyclopedia of Associations* published by Thomson Reuters. In the Portland, Oregon region, access Portland Audubon's *Natural Resources Directory* through www.urbanfauna.org.

Selected Reading and Reference
Favorites from my bookshelves

Abbey, Edward. *Desert Solitaire*. New York: Ballantine, 1968.

Ackerman, Diane. *The Moon by Whale Light*. New York: Random House, 1991.

Alarcón, Francisco X. *Snake Poems*. San Francisco: Chronicle Books, 1992.

Botkin, Daniel, *Our Natural History*. New York: Putnam, 1995.

Carlisle, Andrea. *The Riverhouse Stories*. Corvallis: Calyx, 1986.

Coch, Maryjo. *Bird Egg Feather Nest*. San Francisco: Collins, 1994.

Cody, Robin. *Voyage of a Summer Sun: Canoeing the Columbia River*. New York: Knopf, 1995.

Daniel, John and Larry N. Olson. *Oregon Rivers*. Englewood: Westcliffe, 1997.

Daniel, John. *The Trail Home*. New York: Pantheon, 1992.

----------(editor). *Wild Song: Poems of the Natural World*. Athens: University of Georgia Press, 1998.

Dillard, Annie. *Pilgrim at Tinker Creek*. New York: Harper & Row, 1974.

Gil, Patricio Robles. *Wildlife Spectacles*. Cemex Books on Nature, 2003.

Goode, David. *Wild in London*. London: Michael Joseph London, 1986.

Hill, Jen. *An Exhilaration of Wings*. New York: Viking, 1999.

Hiss, Tony. *The Experience of Place*. New York: Alfred Knopf, 1990.

Holmgren, Virginia C. *The Way of the Hummingbird: In Legend, History and Today's Gardens*. Santa Barbara: Capra Press, 1986.

Hubbell, Sue. *A Country Year: Living the Questions*. New York: Harper & Row, 1986.

Lear, Linda. *Rachel Carson: Witness for Nature*. New York: Henry Holt, 1997.

Little, Charles. *Greenways for America*. Baltimore: Johns Hopkins University Press, 1990.

Lopez, Barry. *About this Life*. New York: Alfred A. Knopf, 1998.

Louv, Richard. *Last Child in the Woods*. Chapel Hill: Algonquin, 2005.

Matthiessen, Peter. *The Birds of Heaven*. New York: North Point Press, 2001.

McKibben, Bill. *The End of Nature*. New York: Random House, 1999.

McKinney, Sam. *Reach of Tide, Ring of History*. Portland: Oregon Historical Society, 1987.

Morine, David E. *Good Dirt: Confessions of a Conservationist*. New York: Ballantine, 1990.

Nelson, Peter. *Treehouses*. New York: Houghton Mifflin, 1994.

Quammen, David. *Natural Acts: A Sidelong View of Science and Nature*. New York: Dell, 1995.

Steinhart, Peter. *Tracks in the Sky*. Vancouver: Raincoast, 1987.

Thaxter, Celia. *An Island Garden, with illustrations by Childe Hassam*. Boston: Houghton Mifflin, 1988.

Williams, Terry Tempest. *Refuge*. New York: Pantheon, 1991.

----------. *An Unspoken Hunger: Stories from the Field*. New York: Pantheon, 1994.

Zepatos, Thalia and Elizabeth Kaufman. *Women For a Change: A Grassroots Guide to Activism and Politics*. New York: Facts on File, 1995.

Art/Photography

Boice, Judith (editor). *Mother Earth: Through the Eyes of Women Photographers and Writers*. San Francisco: Sierra Club, 1992.

Hinchman, Hannah. *A Trail Through Leaves: The Journal as a Path to Place*. New York: W.W. Norton, 1997.

Robinson, Duncan. *Worldview: The Watercolor Diaries of Tony Foster*. Seattle: Frye Art Museum, 2000.

Wolfe, Art. *Pacific Northwest: Land of Light and Water*. Seattle: Sasquatch Books, 1998.

Children

Cannon, Janell. *Stellaluna*. San Diego: Harcourt Brace, 1993.

Carson, Rachel. *The Sense of Wonder*. New York: Harper Collins, 1998.

Dannenmaier, Molly. *A Child's Garden: Enchanting Outdoor Spaces for Children and Parents*. Simon & Shuster, 1998.

Lyons, Daniel. *The Tree*. Bellevue: Illumination Arts, 2002.

Ryder, Joanne. *Dancers in the Garden*. San Francisco: Sierra Club, 1992.

Smucker, Anna Egan. *No Star Nights*. New York: Alfred A. Knopf, 1989.

Field Guides/Reference

Hay, Keith. *The Lewis & Clark Columbia River Water Trail,* Portland: Timber Press, 2004.

Houck, Michael C. and M.J. Cody (editors). *Wild in the City: A Guide to Portland's Natural Areas*. Portland: Oregon Historical Society Press, 2000.

Jones, Philip N. *Bicycling the Backroads: Northwest Oregon*. Seattle: The Mountaineers, 1992.

----------. *Canoe and Kayak Routes of NW Oregon and SW Washington*. Seattle: The Mountaineers, 2007.

Lopez, Barry (editor). *Home Ground: Language for an American Landscape.* San Antonio: Trinity University Press, 2006.

McArthur, Lewis A. *Oregon Geographic Names.* Portland: Oregon Historical Society Press, 1992.

McGavin, George C. *American Nature Guides: Insects.* New York: Smithmark, 1992.

McGee, Peter. *Kayak Routes of the Pacific Northwest Coast.* Vancouver: Greystone Books, 2004.

McLean, Cheryl & Clint Brown. *Oregon's Quiet Waters.* Corvallis: Jackson Creek Press, 1987.

National Geographic Society. *Field Guide to the Birds of North America.* Washington, D.C.: National Geographic, 1989.

Nehls, Harry B. *Familiar Birds of the Northwest.* Portland: Portland Audubon Society, 1983.

Niering, William A. *Wetlands.* New York: Alfred A. Knopf, 1988.

Sibley, David Allen. *The Sibley Guide to Birds.* New York: Alfred A. Knopf, 2000.

Spellenberg, Richard. *Audubon Field Guide to N.A. Wildflowers.* New York: Alfred A. Knopf, 1979.

Terres, John K. *Audubon Encyclopedia of N.A. Birds.* New York: Alfred A. Knopf, 1980.

Whitaker, John, O. Jr. *Audubon Field Guide to N.A. Mammals.* New York: Alfred A. Knopf, 1980.

Whitney, Stephen. *Western Forests.* New York: Alfred A. Knopf, 1988.

Acknowledgments

This book took seven years to evolve into its present shape, first as journal entries, Conservancy newsletter articles, then essays, gradually worked into a cohesive set of stories. I owe a great debt of gratitude to the many people who helped me find my way.

Sharon Wood Wortman, Evelyn Adams, Bob Wilson and Cecilia Haack read drafts of the first two chapters and offered unbridled encouragement.

In John Daniel's nature essay writing class, I discovered I was in fact writing *essays,* and how they ought to develop. John's talent, caring and inestimable knowledge of the natural world helped me sort out "the good stuff."

Linny and Dennis Stovall helped me to realize what I was really writing about.

My late mother, Gertrude Puhala Matrazzo, generously allowed me to share the intimate family story of my father's death.

I'd like to thank the Northwest Writing Institute of Lewis and Clark College for the Walden Fellowship Award, which gave me six weeks at Elizabeth Udall's secluded mountain cabin at Walden Farm to complete the first draft.

Mike Houck first opened my eyes to urban wildlife, and guided me to finding a place for myself. Elizabeth Udall read every word and offered enthusiasm and insight. Alison Highberger nourished me with marvelous dinners, gifts of other nature writing and assurance that this was more than a regional story.

Thanks to New York agent Julian Bach who represented this book for a time, encouraged me to write more about Braddock, and suggested two additional chapters and the Appendix.

Many professional environmentalists and grassroots conservation activists—far too many to mention here—gave me knowledge, understanding and sometimes a desperately-needed shoulder to lean on through these adventures.

When the manuscript languished in a file drawer, Mary Forst nudged me into getting it into print. Vicki Lind and my Creative Job Club networking colleagues, especially Jill Kelly and Gigi Rosenberg, supported the process.

Most of all I would like to thank all the people whose names are woven throughout this book for allowing me to tell their stories.

Literature Cited

Bach, Richard. *Illusions: The Adventures of a Reluctant Messiah.* New York: Dell, 1977, pg. 65.

Goodall, Jane. *National Geographic,* " A Message from Jane Goodall," 188:6, pg. 129.

Pyle, Robert Michael. *The Thunder Tree.* Guilford, CT: Lyons Press, 1998.

Roszak, Theodore, Mary E. Gomes and Allen D. Kanner, *Ecopsychology: Restoring the Earth, Healing the Mind.* San Francisco: Sierra Club Books, 1995, pg. 258.

Trimble, Stephen, Foreward by Edward Abbey. *Blessed by Light: Visions of the Colorado Plateau.* Layton, UT: Gibbs M. Smith, 1986, pg. xvi.

Ulman, Liv. *Changing.* New York: Knopf, 1977, page 106.

About the Author

© Aly Bleiler

DONNA MATRAZZO is a science, environmental and history writer whose work has appeared in numerous publications, on PBS and the Discovery Channel, and in national park visitor centers and museums around the country. She is one of the founders of the Sauvie Island Conservancy and the Oregon Ocean Paddling Society, and volunteers for Portland Audubon, Willamette Riverkeeper and the Lower Columbia River Water Trail. She has lived on Sauvie Island for 20 years. View her website at www.donnamatrazzo.com

Printed in the United States
127377LV00003B/1-144/P